'More than a decade after the financial crisis, *Split* is a timely reminder of the most important divide that runs through the global economy, and how working people can organise to take back control of their lives. Clearly-argued, incisive and accessible, this book should be required reading for activists everywhere.'
Grace Blakeley, author of *Stolen: How to Save the World from Financialisaton*

'This book is essential reading for making sense of society, digging into the realities of class for young people today. It shows how deeply Britain is shaped by class, while also charting out ways people can collectively change this.'
Jamie Woodcock, co-author of *The Gig Economy: A Critical Introduction*

'Neoliberal ideology hinges on the claim that class no longer matters – but as inequalities rise to unprecedented extremes, class divisions are now more prominent than ever. *Split* is packed with fresh insights into how class structures our world, and what we can do to build a fairer economy.'
Jason Hickel, author of *The Divide: Global Inequality from Conquest to Free Markets*

'*Split* is an essential introduction to the dimensions of class division that have shaped the modern world. If you want to understand why society has become ever more polarised, and how we might go about fixing it, read this book.'
Laurie Macfarlane, Economics Editor at openDemocracy and co-author of *Rethinking the Economics of Land and Housing*

'Intelligent, lucid and engaging from beginning to end, Tippet's book is a must-read for those who want to learn the root cause of pervasive inequality that defines our world.'
Brett Scott, author of *The Heretic's Guide to Global Finance: Hacking the Future of Money*

Outspoken
Series Editor: Neda Tehrani

Platforming underrepresented voices; intervening in important political issues; revealing powerful histories and giving voice to our experiences; Outspoken is a book series unlike any other. Unravelling debates on sex ed and masculinity, feminism and class, and work and borders, Outspoken has the answers to the questions you're asking. These are books that dissent.

Also available:

Mask Off
Masculinity Redefined
JJ Bola

Behind Closed Doors
Sex Education Transformed
Natalie Fiennes

Feminism, Interrupted
Disrupting Power
Lola Olufemi

Split

Class Divides Uncovered

Ben Tippet

First published 2020 by Pluto Press
345 Archway Road, London N6 5AA

www.plutobooks.com

British Library Cataloguing in Publication Data
A catalogue record for this book is available from the British Library

ISBN   978 0 7453 4021 0   Paperback
ISBN   978 1 7868 0595 9   PDF eBook
ISBN   978 1 7868 0597 3   Kindle eBook
ISBN   978 1 7868 0596 6   EPUB eBook

This book is printed on paper suitable for recycling and made
from fully managed and sustained forest sources. Logging, pulping
and manufacturing processes are expected to conform to the
environmental standards of the country of origin.

Typeset by Stanford DTP Services, Northampton, England

Simultaneously printed in the United Kingdom and United States of
America

Contents

Acknowledgements

I would like to thank Neda Tehrani and everyone at Pluto Press for making this series a reality and for giving young, first time writers a chance to publish and call a book their own. No book however just belongs to the author, and this one would not have been possible without the incredible support of my friends, family and the brilliant young people who I have interviewed along the way. Thank you to my friends, who have shared with me so many inspiring conversations, protests, occupations, lessons, flats, houses, nights out and all the moments that make life worth living. In particular, I would like to thank the friends that helped develop the ideas and edit the text for this book – Jack Browne, Jeff Moxom, Laetitia Bouhelier, Lydia Hughes, Jamie Woodcock, Thomas Rabensteiner, Franck Magennis, Hannah Slydel, Anna and Peter Fiennes, Özlem Onaran, Sam Adams, Matt Dickinson, Ollie Gaughran, Aidan Harper, Ines Heck, Tom Welsh, Joey Martin, Jonny Harper and Charlie Fox. Thank you to all the inspiring young people who I interviewed for this book and for the political spirit and critical voices that can be found in any classroom. Most importantly, I would like to thank Natalie Fiennes who has supported me every step of the way in writing this book and without whom I would still be stressing over the wording of a single line. And lastly, thank you to my family – to my parents for always supporting me in the choices I make, and in particular to my brother, Sam, who from a young age taught me how to be political and to stand up for the things you believe in.

Introduction: Class is a lucrative British export

Britain is famed for its rigid class hierarchies. From mustachioed gentlemen with stiff upper lips to industrial workers with dirty overalls and parochial accents, the British class system has been neatly stereotyped and typecast into the national story. This rosy and nostalgic picture of class relations has been retold to the world for over a hundred years.

At the time of writing, the most expensive TV show ever made is *The Crown*, a ten-part Netflix drama detailing the customs, relationships and power battles in the highest echelons of Britain's class system. The series focuses almost exclusively on the lives of the Royal Family and elite politicians, who exist in a separate world to the rest of society. In the words of the late Harry Leslie-Smith, Second World War veteran and international Twitter star, '*The Crown* is like an expensive painting in which the only subjects in focus are the rich and privileged.'

The director of *The Crown*, Stephen Daldry, seems less captivated with the glittering allure of royalty, and more with a romantic representation of the British class system, having directed another famous drama, at the other end of the class ladder: *Billy Elliot*. The film recounts the story of a young working-class boy who aspires to become a ballet dancer. Set in the north-east of England, against the backdrop of the 1984–5 miners' strike, it dramatises the hardship faced by coal miners

1

in their struggle to defend their livelihoods. The strike was a watershed moment in British class history, due to both its size (it was the country's largest strike since 1926, involving over 142,000 mineworkers) and the long lasting impact it has had on working class political power.[1] The historic importance of the dispute is captured in a poignant scene towards the end of the film. Billy Elliot's father, Jackie, is a single parent and a coal miner out on strike. Having not earned an income for months, he is struggling to put food on the table, let alone pay for each of Billy's 50p ballet lessons. When Billy is accepted for an audition at the Royal Ballet School in London, but cannot afford the bus fare down, his father is forced to make a choice between his child's future and the struggle of his community.

In the end, Jackie breaks the strike. Returning to work, he is met by a crowd of strikers who have formed a picket line to keep the mine closed. In the crowd is Billy's older brother, Tony, who among the shouting and heckling of the crowd, spots his father trying to the break the strike. Stunned and furious, he pushes over a police officer and chases after his dad, before shouting in desperation, 'You can't do this. Not now, not after all this time!' Jackie responds by falling to the floor, 'We're finished son.'

Audiences from around the world have an insatiable appetite for these romantic displays of Britain's class hierarchy. *The Crown* will be released on Netflix over the next decade, while *Billy Elliot* is now an on-stage musical, touring the world from Korea to the US. With *Downton Abbey*, *Victoria* and *Call the Midwife* as popular additions, class is a lucrative British export. These programmes have one thing in common: they represent a nostalgic vision of class from bygone and simpler times. This reflects the widespread belief that class is something of the past – that it doesn't

---

1 Jacobus Hermanus Antonius van der Velden, *Strikes Around the World, 1968–2005: Case-studies of 15 Countries* (Amsterdam: Amsterdam University Press, 2007).

neatly apply to the present or hold as an appropriate vision of the future. And even in those rare cases where class is used to explain some major political event (think Brexit or Trump), it is always based around the old stereotype of the working class as a white, male, industrial worker. To think seriously about class today we need to shake off this nostalgia. The best way to do this is to go back over recent history and ask why our understanding of class has not kept up with the times?

The new world order

After a year of strike action, the miners were defeated by Margaret Thatcher's government. The pits were closed down and whole communities were left without work. At its peak, half a million people worked in Britain's coal industry. Today there are almost none.[2] The closure of the coal mines was one part of an enormous restructuring of the whole of the UK economy. In what is now referred to as 'deindustrialisation', since 1985 nearly 2.5 million jobs in coal, steel, textiles, car and shipbuilding either disappeared or moved to countries in the Global South.[3]

The effect of this scale of job loss on the working classes in the UK was profound. Not only did it plunge families into poverty, but there was a huge rise in homelessness, addiction and long-term unemployment in these old industrial areas. Many of the communities have never recovered. The lack of investment, attention and care given is a deep wound in British history. And perhaps most importantly, deindustrialisation has seen the

---

2   Christina Beatty and Stephen Fothergill, *Jobs, Welfare and Austerity: how the destruction of industrial Britain casts a shadow over the present-day public finances*, project report (Sheffield: Centre for Regional, Economic and Social Research, Sheffield Hallam University, 2016).

3   Ibid., p. 4.

demise of the power and influence of working class organisations, embodied most by the trade union movement. Following the defeat of the miners in 1984–5, trade union membership has been in terminal decline. In 1985, 45.3 per cent of the British workforce was in a trade union. Today, only 23 per cent are. The lack of union representation is particularly stark for the young, as less than 5 per cent of all trade union members are under 25, despite this group making up 14 per cent of all workers.[4] When looking at it from the perspective of British trade unions, Jackie's 'We're finished son' reads like a collective epitaph.

These major economic changes did not just occur in the UK. Jobs throughout the Global North were either destroyed or relocated to countries in the Global South, where workers were paid less and placed under more exploitative working conditions. When we talk about this kind of scale of change, happening over decades, and involving billions of individual lives, it can be hard to imagine how our own individual lives and choices fit into the story. History is filled with these types of great transformations: from the collapse of Rome to the rise and fall of the British Empire. Within each of these eras, there exists a dominant ideology, or a set of ideas that govern us. These ideas, principles and values guide the common sense of the fundamental questions in life – how we should do politics, who should be doing it, and ultimately what it means to live a good life.

So, what is the name of the era we are living under now and what does that have to do with class? The period that was ushered in during the 1980s, and the one that still holds sway across the world today (albeit not without serious contestation) has a name: neo-liberalism. It has created the world today, including our nostalgic class visions. To really understand how

---

4   www.ft.com/content/3f6e9d7c-98bb-11e7-a652-cde3f882dd7b (last accessed 09/ 2019).

and why, we have to get to grips with the key aspect of the ideology – the idea that society should be organised around individual competition.

Billy Elliot is at its heart a moral parable about neo-liberalism and the power of the competitive individual. At the end of the film (spoiler alert), Billy goes to his audition and successfully wins a place at the Royal Ballet School. He leaves the poverty and bitter industrial disputes of his working class community and moves to London, where he has the opportunity to start a new and better life for himself. The message is clear: those who have talent and work hard, no matter where they come from, can achieve their dreams and become successful individuals. To do this though, they must leave behind silly notions that they belong to a class, or that working together with other people from your class can improve things. Through individual competition, Billy succeeds. Through collective struggle, his community fails.

This idea that class does not matter anymore, that it does not fit with the times, is a central component of neo-liberalism. As the world changed, and the future was placed firmly in the hands of the individual, our understanding of class has not been updated. It's like the expression we say to children who are pulling funny faces – 'If the wind changes, it will stick like that'. With the changes of neo-liberalism, our collective understanding of class has remained stuck in the past, crystallised in the 80s.

Does class matter?

There is, however, a fundamental problem with neo-liberal ideology. Its central premise – that class doesn't really matter – is an illusion that does not hold up to serious interrogation. Just because we have not been talking about class, does not mean it has magically disappeared. Sure, the institutional power of the working class has diminished, but arguably this shows class has become more important – not less. As we shall see throughout this book, this is because class is like a see saw: the decline of working class power has been directly tied to the rising success of the other side of the coin: the elite class, or to give it another name, the capitalist class.

Part of the reason we do not talk about class as much as we used to is due to the success of neo-liberal ideology itself. The message that we get on in life through competition, and that class no longer matters, has itself been used as a tool by the elites to undermine the collective power of the working class.

To see how this works, consider the 2017 Oscar winning horror film, *Get Out* – a chilling satire about the underlying racism of a supposedly colour-blind liberal America. The story begins with a young happy couple in New York: Chris, a black photographer, is invited by his white girlfriend Rose to meet her parents at their country mansion for a weekend visit. Chris is initially concerned that her white parents will harbour racist views towards him, 'Do they know I'm black?', but his concerns are shrugged off by Rose, 'No, should they? . . . my parents are not racist. My dad would have voted for Obama a third time if he could!'

Chris agrees to go, but after arriving at the isolated country house, strange things start to happen. While Rose and her parents continue to profess their colour blindness, Chris notices the signs of a clear and violent racial divide. Acting particularly strangely are the two black servants who work for the white family on the estate. Rose's dad shrugs off the fact that he has black servants as an unfortunate coincidence, 'I know it looks bad but . . . ' However, when Chris tries to make conversation, neither servant reacts, behaving instead like lobotomised, isolated robots. Similarly, at a party the next day,

Chris approaches the only other black guest with a comradely, 'Good to see another brother around here', only to be greeted by a blank and unfriendly response. As the film develops (another spoiler alert!), we see that the family's attempt to pretend race no longer matters, despite its obvious presence, is actually a designed tactic by Rose and her family to ensnare Chris into a trap. Their real aim is to hypnotise him and transform him into another one of their helpers.

People may constantly claim that they don't see it, that it doesn't really exist (at least not anymore) and make excuses for its seemingly obvious effects. But as we can see from *Get Out*, this does not make the racial divide disappear, or make it safe for those at the sharp, receiving end of it. The image of a happy, post-racial family simply lures Chris into a situation where he is isolated and unable to communicate with those who might be able to help him, and who might be on his side.

This point is very similar for class under neo-liberalism: the constant repetition that 'class no longer matters' by elites has been used to undermine the collective power of the working class, or to draw the metaphor to its final conclusion – to individualise and lobotomise them for their own ends.

There are countless examples of how this is done. A common tactic straight out of the neo-liberal playbook is to get us all to see ourselves as competitive players in a system where we win or lose depending on how hard we work. A game where we are told to valorise the winners and judge those who will not or cannot compete and might therefore be skiving off the system. George Osborne, the ex-Chancellor of the Exchequer and current Editor of the Evening Standard, summarised this tactic best in two lines he gave in a 2012 radio interview, justifying a fresh £10 billion round of cuts to the welfare budget: 'The rich will be asked to pay a greater share. But it is a "delusion" to think that taxes on the rich will solve the problem. It is unfair that people listening to this programme going out to work, see the neighbour next door with the blinds down because they are on benefits.'[5]

The purpose of these messages is to turn people against each other – an age-old trick of divide and conquer for the twenty-first century. It does not matter if the blinds are down because your neighbour has been working a night shift. Osborne and his class can sit at home, behind their family-made curtains (Osborne's father is a leading retailer in the luxury fabric industry after all) in the safe knowledge that the anger and derision is not being turned against them.

Millennial socialism

The glistening sheen of neo-liberal ideology is starting to wear off. This started with the 2008 financial crisis, and the strange dissonant decade we have just lived through, full of electrifying political moments against the backdrop of a dull, sluggish economic 'recovery'. Class is coming back onto the agenda, as the divisions that have always been there are becoming harder to ignore.

You cannot talk about class and the economy without understanding some of the ideas of Karl Marx. Writing in the nineteenth century, his theories about class, power and capitalism have shaped the world more than any other thinker on the subject. As both an intellectual and a campaigner, Marx tried to understand how capitalism really works. For him, capitalism is an exploitative economic system that divides humans into classes based on their role in the economy. By their very defi-

---

5   From 2012 interview on the *Today* programme. www.theguardian.com/politics/blog/2012/oct/08/curtains-closed-blinds-down-george-osborne, (last accessed 09/2019).

nition, the ruling classes, those that own and control property, are in unceasing conflict with the working classes, those that have to sell their labour for a wage. For Marx, this class conflict becomes a central and inescapable force of history. Whether we like it or not, class is something we are all shaped by.

For its critics, 'Marxism', 'socialism' and 'communism' seems to occupy a contradictory position in the history of economic thought – his ideas being treated as both dangerously radical and historically outdated. Marx is a controversial figure. This is in part due to the cruelty and violence committed by people in his name, from the killing fields of the Cambodian Dictator Pol Pot, to the millions who died under Stalin's totalitarian regime. A quick look at the history of Marxist thought shows that there is a strong democratic and pluralistic tradition that is not only deeply critical of these authoritarian turns, but which also has a wealth of knowledge to offer all of us that live under capitalism and feel the sharp forces of the class divide.

One group that clearly feel these forces is the young. Under the banner of 'millennial socialism', Marx and some of his ideas are having somewhat of a revival. In 2016 a YouGov poll found that young people in Britain between the ages of 18 to 24 were 18 per cent more likely to have a favourable rather than unfavourable view of socialism. When it came to their attitudes on capitalism, almost the complete opposite was true.[6] While one poll at one point in time is not the most reliable source for gauging people's opinions, this result has been repeated in polls of young people in wealthy capitalist countries across the word. In the US, a YouGov poll found that 18–29 year olds had a 43 per cent favourable opinion of socialism, compared to just 26 per

---

6   Will Dahlgreen, 'British people keener on socialism than capitalism', YouGov (2016) https://yougov.co.uk/topics/politics/articles-reports/2016/02/23/british-people-view-socialism-more-favourably-capi (last accessed 09/2019).

cent that did not.[7] In Australia, a right wing think tank commissioned a survey with YouGov Galaxy, and to their horror found that 58 per cent of millennials favoured socialism to capitalism, and 59 percent thought that 'capitalism has failed and government should exercise more control of the economy'.[8]

Further polling also seems to suggest that a favourable attitude towards socialism is grounded in a desire to transform the economic structure of society. In the voting booths, the young seem attracted to parties that offer policies along more radical socialist lines. For example, in the UK 2017 general election, 66 per cent of 18–19 year olds voted for the Labour Party, which had just adopted a radical economic programme, while only 19 per cent of over 70 year olds pledged their support for Labour.[9] If it were just the votes of the under 25s that counted in that election, the right wing Conservative Party would not have won a single seat.[10]

Young people are looking for transformative change. Throughout this book, we will see why, by telling the story of the economic reality many currently face. A Marxist analysis will not just help us understand how we got here, but also how progressive change can come about. As Marx said, 'Philosophers have hitherto only interpreted the world in various ways; the point is to change it'.

---

7   William Jordan, 'Democrats more divided on socialism', YouGov (2016) https://today.yougov.com/topics/politics/articles-reports/2016/01/28/democrats-remain-divided-socialism (last accessed 09/2019).
8   Tom Switzer and Charles Jacobs, *Millennials and socialism: Australian youth are lurching to the left* (The Centre for Independent Studies, Policy Paper 7, 2018).
9   Chris Curtis, 'How Britain voted at the 2017 general election', YouGov (2017) https://yougov.co.uk/topics/politics/articles-reports/2017/06/13/how-britain-voted-2017-general-election (last accessed 09/2019).
10 www.ft.com/content/cbed81fc-3b56-11e9-9988-28303f70fcff socialism (last accessed 09/2019).

INTRODUCTION

A bundle of sticks

Out of the vacuum of neo-liberalism, the right have spotted an opportunity. They have realised that working class voices have been forgotten, and are using a language of class to further their political project. Unlike the distinction between capital and labour discussed in this book, they claim that the real class divide is between a left-behind traditional working class, and the liberal metropolitan elite, who have betrayed them by throwing in their lot with immigrants and minority groups. It's a narrative that links straight back to our nostalgic image of class: a longing for a simple past where the working class is clearly defined as industrial, white men.

It is time to reclaim class. To do this we need to know how twenty-first century work, life and politics are defined by class division. Most crucially, we need to turn the neo-liberal theory of success on its head, and show that individual competition has not turned us into talented ballet dancers – if anything, it has turned us into lobotomised servants. To bring us out of the current crisis and on the road to individual and collective success, we need an organised, inclusive working class movement to take on the power of the wealthy elite. While the rich use their money to buy influence and fame, working class voices are best heard when spoken collectively and in solidarity with each other. This is an old and simple truth that goes back thousands of years and was put best in a famous fable from Aesop, an ancient Greek slave and one of history's greatest storytellers.

A long time ago, there was a father and his three quarrelling sons. As the man grew old and approached his last days, he ordered his sons to bring him a bundle of sticks so he could teach them a crucial lesson about life. Tying the bundle together, he asked each of his sons to break the sticks in two. None of them could do it. The old man then untied the bundle and asked again, this time holding each stick one at a time. Within a few moments, and without a single drop of sweat, every stick had been snapped. 'You see my point', said the Old Man. 'Individually, you are easy to break, but together you are invincible'.

Chapter 1

The split: Capital and labour

The hippopotamus is one of the deadliest animals in the world. This may come as a surprise given that this leisurely beast spends most of its life serenely bathing in muddy rivers and ponds, despite not being able to swim. Such a zen appearance, however, masks what is at heart an incredibly aggressive animal. Their teeth are sharp, and despite weighing well over a tonne, they will easily outrun a human. This deadly concoction of might and aggression leads to the tragic death of thousands of people across the world each year.

The hippo's image of power is likely the reason why 'hippo' is the name given to armoured police vans in South Africa. Trevor Noah, the South African comedian who fronts the popular US political TV comedy *The Daily Show*, remembers their lurking presence while growing up under apartheid: 'The police would swoop in out of nowhere, riding in armoured personnel carriers – hippos, we called them – tanks with enormous tires and slotted holes in the side of the vehicle to fire their guns out of. You didn't mess with a hippo. You saw one, you ran.'[1]

---

1   Trevor Noah, 'Trevor Noah on Growing Up in South Africa Under Apartheid', Lit Hub (2016). https://lithub.com/trevor-noah-on-growing-up-in-south-africa-under-apartheid (last accessed 09/2019).

We start our story of class in South Africa – the most economically unequal country on the planet – because at its heart, class is an attempt to frame and make sense of the deep inequalities of our world. South Africa shows us how class is, like the hippo, a global, powerful and sometimes dangerous phenomenon.

Marikana is a small mining town in the dusty north-west of South Africa. Home to around 30,000 people, the craggy landscape has earned it the name, 'Rooikoppies' – which translates from Afrikaans as 'red hills'. The region is beautiful, but this is not why the town Marikana has become a household name. Marikana sits at the centre of South Africa's platinum industry, housing a large mine that provides work for most of the families that live there.

Before August 2012, the world did not know about these miners and their families. They were a small and invisible cog in the vast machine of a global economy. Yet that month the Marikana miners threw a spanner in the works of this great machine, leading to a catastrophic series of events that the world could not ignore.

A story of capital and labour

It started on Thursday 9 August, when the miners organised a meeting on top of one of the red hills overlooking Marikana. They were angry, earning a tiny wage for gruelling and back-breaking work deep in the tunnels of the mine. A typical day would be spent underground for 12–14 hours in a hot, stagnant environment filled with silica dust dispersed by explosions in the mines. Simply breathing in these conditions puts miners at particular risk of contracting tuberculosis, a disease which was virtually wiped out in the UK in the 1980s, but is the leading

14

cause of death in South Africa, where it kills on average ten people an hour.[2]

Each miner in 2012 was making just under 200 rand a day, the equivalent of £10. It is little wonder then that the meeting ended with a unanimous agreement: they decided to go on strike until their pay had been tripled. Given that the mines were owned by Lonmin, a multinational mining corporation headquartered in London, but operating in South Africa, this demand had to travel 5,635 miles until it reached the people who ultimately held the power to grant it. It's fair to say that Lonmin's managers and owners did not receive the message well.

Upon first hearing about the dispute, a Lonmin executive wrote an internal memo advising the company to sack the strikers and call in the police, stating that the company's priority was 'getting people arrested'.[3] Another wrote to the South African minister for mineral resources, asking her to 'bring the full might of the state to bear on the situation'.[4] Lonmin didn't want to increase the miner's pay for a simple reason: it would hurt profits. Like most major multinational corporations, Lonmin is a public company, which means its shares are traded on a stock exchange. Each quarter (i.e. four times a year) the company's profits are taken and distributed to the shareholders in what is known as a dividend. In the four years leading up to 2012, as platinum flowed out of Marikana and into the world market, $607 million came flooding in back into shareholders pockets in the form of these dividends.[5]

2   Anna Vassall, 'Tuberculosis South Africa Perspectives', (Post-2015 Development Agenda) www.copenhagenconsensus.com/sites/default/files/south_africa_tuberculosis_resouce_packet.pdf (last accessed 09/2019).

3   www.theguardian.com/world/2015/may/19/marikana-massacre-untold-story-strike-leader-died-workers-rights (last accessed 09/2019).

4   Ibid.

5   https://londonminingnetwork.org/2019/03/press-release-lonmins-profits-rise-as-marikana-community-continues-to-suffer (last accessed 09/2019).

Most multinational corporations like Lonmin leave the day-to-day running of the business to a team of managers. Lonmin's CEO at the time, Ian Farmer, refused to meet the strikers. In the dry language of business speak, he argued that the company simply couldn't afford to increase the pay, 'Revenue at the time was not generating the sufficient margin for us to be generating the cash needed'.[6] The CEO did, however, find the cash to pay himself: taking home £933,605 in 2012 alone. In other words, he was making a miner's annual salary in one single day.[7]

What exists here is a complicated set of power relations between two groups of people. On one side are the miners who sell their labour to the company for a wage. On the other side are the shareholders and the managers, who control the daily work lives of the miners. They make the decisions over who works, where they work, how they work, who they work with and when they work. But most importantly they distribute the money, controlling how much everyone receives in pay.

It is no accident that the managers and owners of Lonmin are rich and the miners are poor. The relationship between the two groups is unambiguously defined by exploitation – the managers and owners benefitting economically from the others by controlling and appropriating their labouring activity. Exploitation is not something static, but represents an ongoing interaction between the lives of disparate people.

Class starts with this great split down the middle of the economy – between those who own and control the workplace, and those who have to sell their labour to survive. Throughout the book we will call this class split the 'capital-labour relation'.

---

6   www.thebureauinvestigates.com/stories/2013-11-24/questions-raised-about-role-of-british-company-in-south-african-mining-massacre (last accessed 09/2019).
7   www.lonmin.com/reports/2012/online_annual_report_2012/pdfs/Lonmin_AR2012.pdf (last accessed 03/2019).

But unlike a relationship with a friend, this is based on a fundamental conflict over who gets what. And this conflict can easily spark into violence.

'We need to act such that we kill this thing'

The week that followed the declaration of the strike was tumultuous. From Friday to Monday, violent clashes between the strikers on one side and a motley crew of Lonmin, the National Union of Mineworkers, South Africa's African National Congress (ANC) and the police on the other, led to the deaths of two security guards, two workers, three strikers and two police officers.

By the following Thursday, the miners found themselves back on top of the hill where they had started. Yet this time they were greater in number and were at a critical turning point of the dispute, having heard that officials of Lonmin would finally agree to negotiate for higher wages, if the strikers were willing to return back to work. This time they were not meeting alone: lurking beneath them was a massive, armed police force. The previous night more than 550 police officers had descended on Marikana, armed to the teeth with hippos, helicopters and 4,000 rounds of live ammunition. In an ominous sign of their intentions, the police had also brought along several mortuary vans with the capacity to take away dozens of dead bodies.

From 9 a.m. to 3:30 p.m. around 3,000 of the miners waited while a small group tried to negotiate. The dispute was at a knife-edge and all anticipated some kind of offer. Yet when the negotiators finally returned, they brought only bad news: 'the life of a black person in Africa is so cheap . . . They will kill us, they will finish us and then they will replace us and continue to pay wages that cannot change black people's lives'.[8] It was then that the police, in their hippos, started to move, laying out barbed wire around the workers to close them in.[9] In protest, a small group of miners came down from the hill to argue that a gap should be left open, so the miners could leave in peace, but the police responded by raising their guns. According to one eye witness, 'the first person who started to shoot was a soldier in a Hippo, and he never fired a warning shot, he just shot straight at us'.[10] Within a few minutes, 16 miners had been murdered and many more injured.

This was all captured on TV cameras from behind the police lines – videos which still eerily circulate on YouTube. Outside the view of the cameras, a group of miners made their way to a small rocky outcrop to the west of the hill, finding shelter among the bushes and trees. This hiding place would quickly be turned into a killing field. Police in helicopters and hippos encircled the group, and under the cover of those trees and shrubs, executed another 14 people, often at point blank range.[11] It was to be the bloodiest hour in post-apartheid South Africa. Before the dust had settled, 78 miners were wounded. 34 had been killed.

What motivated such an aggressive response from the police? The Marikana massacre was not simply a random act of state violence. In the lead up to the massacre, senior police officers and managers at Lonmin had met to plan their next course of action. The police chief, Lt Gen Mbombo, was recorded at the meeting as being eagerly in favour of trying to shut down

---

8   www.theguardian.com/world/2015/may/19/marikana-massacre-untold-story-strike-leader-died-workers-rights

9   Peter Alexander, 'Marikana autopsy of a cold-blooded massacre', *Journal des anthropologues*, 136–7, (2014): 353–69.

10   Ibid.

11   www.iol.co.za/news/the-murder-fields-of-marikana-1373581 (last accessed 09/2019).

the strikes, 'We need to act such that we kill this thing'.[12] In agreement, a Lonmin executive responded by complimenting the police force for their lethal firepower, 'The ones that impress me [are] the snipers'.[13] The endgame was clear: they wanted to finish off the strike for good and by any means necessary.

While the extent of the violence may be exceptional, this episode tells us about the discipline that is used to maintain the capital-labour split. When the miners tried to make workplace decisions, they challenged the established hierarchy between these two camps. Such a challenge had to be met with a response. In its bluntest form, enforcement comes out of the barrel of a gun. However, less violent and more effective strategies are routinely pursued. The most common one, probably something we will all feel at some point in our lives, is the threat of being fired from your job if you put your head above the parapet. The authorities – schools, police and prisons – are not neutral arbitrators in this relationship. As we shall see throughout this book, more often than not they side with capital to reinforce the capital-labour relation. All of this discipline and control highlights an important aspect of class – there is nothing natural about it. Like baking a cake, the right conditions need to be maintained for the class hierarchy to remain stable.

How did the miners of Marikana become miners?

The capital-labour relation has not always existed. As we shall see in the next chapter, work might feel like an inevitable slog, but in the history of humanity the primary way that people have survived is not by selling their labour to capital. This way of

---

12 www.theguardian.com/world/2015/may/19/marikana-massacre-untold-story-strike-leader-died-workers-rights
13 Ibid.

organising the economy is actually a relatively recent invention. Take for example the following question: how did the miners of Marikana become miners in the first place? While each individual will have their own personal history, their collective story is one shared by people across the world.

The area now known as South Africa before the sixteenth century was an agricultural society made up of farmers, pastoralists, and hunter-gatherers.[14] They did not earn a wage, but rather lived off the land, producing grain and livestock to meet their needs. This would all change with the arrival of European explorers, first from Portugal and later from the Netherlands, England and France. In 1652, the Dutch established Cape Town as a settlement, now the legislative capital. This was seized in 1806 by Britain, inaugurating a sustained and extensive era of colonial expansion in the region.

If there was one man that embodied this era, it would be British colonialist Cecil Rhodes. At the age of 18, he entered the growing mining industry, built around diamonds that were found in South Africa in 1867 (in reality, of course, diamonds had been there for many years before Europeans arrived). Within 20 years Rhodes had capitalised on these gems and established the company, De Beers. De Beers would go on to monopolise the world's rough diamond trade for the next 120 years and still today its diamonds are a global symbol of decadence – the company brands itself as the 'Home of Diamonds Since 1888'. Rhodes' corporate and personal wealth exploded exponentially in tandem with the expansion of the British Empire, as he built riches off the poverty of others. During these decades European powers were occupying, dividing and colonising the

14 John Wright, *Southern Africa before Colonial Times*, Oxford Research Encyclopedias (2017) https://oxfordre.com/africanhistory/africanhistory/view/10.1093/acrefore/9780190277734.001.0001/acrefore-9780190277734-e-92.

whole of the African continent in what has come to be called 'the scramble for Africa'. In South Africa, British colonial forces had violently won power after a series of bloody wars, culminating in the Anglo-Boer War at the end of the century, involving some of the first uses of concentration camps.

By 1896, Cecil Rhodes had become Prime Minister of the Cape and one of the richest men on earth. One of his final acts before he died was passing a law that would help him to accumulate ever-greater wealth and power. His policy would serve as the basis of the infamous Natives Land Act, which came into effect in 1913, a few years after Rhodes had died. At the stroke of a legislative pen, the law severely restricted the land that indigenous Africans could own. Despite making up 67 per cent of the population, they were segregated onto only 7 per cent of agricultural land[15] – the start of the racial apartheid system that would haunt the country over the coming century. The purpose of the law was clear. By seizing the land, Africans would have no choice but to work in the mines and farms owned by European colonists.[16] William Beinart, the Rhodes (named after Cecil Rhodes himself) Professor of Race Relations at the University of Oxford claims, 'The Act did not aim to move black people off the commercial farms but to keep them there as workers'.[17] We can see that the historical descendants of the Marikana miners did not become miners of their own choosing, but ended up there because of global historical forces that dispossessed them of the land they needed to survive. As Cecil Rhodes himself

15   Harvey M. Feinberg, 'The 1913 Natives Land Act in South Africa: Politics, Race, and Segregation in the Early 20th Century', *The International Journal of African Historical Studies* 26, no. 1 (1993): 65–109.
16   John Wright, *Southern Africa before Colonial Times*.
17   William Beinart and Peter Delius, 'The Historical Context and Legacy of the Natives Land Act of 1913', *Journal of Southern African Studies* 40, no. 4 (2014): 667–88.

succinctly put it, the purpose was to 'give them a stimulus in labour'.[18]

Strikes: Results and legacy

The Marikana massacre did not stop the strikers – if anything, it emboldened them. Just the day after the mass killings, Lonmin's finance director, Simon Scott, warned that if the miners did not return to work by Monday, they would all be sacked.[19] His threats fell on deaf ears. The strike continued for another five weeks until they finally won a collective 22 per cent rise in pay – less than their original demand, but still a substantial win.

Retracting your work – i.e. striking – is hugely damaging for profits as it grinds business to a halt. The industrial dispute was said to have cost Lonmin 4.5 billion rand (£335 million) in lost output. Given that owners and managers eventually pay themselves from these profits, Lonmin had no choice in the end but to concede. What happened in Marikana sent shock waves throughout the South African mining industry. Two years later in January 2014, almost 70,000 platinum miners went on strike with the same demand as the Marikana strikers. The dispute would last for five months, making it the largest and most expensive strike in the history of South Africa. Workers gave up £565 million in lost wages, but inflicted £1.2 billion in lost revenues on the companies involved. By June an agreement had been reached: nearly two years on from the massacre, tens of thousands of people had been given the full pay increase that had initially been demanded on that red hill on that summer morning.[20]

---

18   The Natives Land Act of 1913, South African History Online (2013) www.sahistory.org.za/article/natives-land-act-1913 (last accessed 09/2019).

19   www.bbc.co.uk/news/business-19300420 (last accessed 09/2019).

20   www.gov.uk/government/publications/south-africa-platinum-strike-ends-june-2014/south-africa-platinum-strike-ends-june-2014 (last accessed 09/2019).

Class is global

You might be thinking that this example has been cherry-picked in order to highlight the injustice produced by the capital-labour split. But there is nothing exceptional about the class-based inequality within Lonmin. Taking a comparison across the globe, the wages of Marikana miners are actually relatively high and the wealth of Lonmin's owners and managers relatively low. More than half the world's population, 4.3 billion people, earn less than $5 a day – significantly less than the miners of Marikana.[21] Moreover, ranked by the capitalists of the mining industry, Lonmin is a small fish. A few months before the massacre in 2012 a website originally named www.mining.com listed the top 'mining billionaires' in the world at the time. No one on Lonmin's board or management made it onto the list. At the top of the list was Brazil's Eike Fuhrken Batista, worth $32.8 billion at the time, making him the seventh richest man in the world.

What does the story of Marikana tell us about class relations in Britain today? Class is often presented to us as something that is quintessentially British; something that only exists on the playing fields of Eton, in the corridors of Buckingham Palace, and down the back alleys of inner-city estates. What Marikana shows is that the class split between capital and labour, and the inequalities it produces, extends well beyond the borders of the British Isles. Class is global.

As we shall see throughout the rest of this book, many of the features of the Marikana massacre apply to modern Britain: a wealthy capitalist class that still controls and manages our working lives, inequality linked to exploitation, and a government too willing to side with the interests of the rich. More

---

21 Jason Hickel, *The Divide: A Brief Guide to Global Inequality and its Solutions* (William Heinemann, 2017).

than this, the story shows how we cannot understand class in Britain without understanding its relationship to the rest of the world – a relationship that is so often governed by colonial expansion and extraction. While the British Empire may have been consigned to the history books, the class and racial inequalities that sustained it are still being reproduced each day. Take for instance the example of mining used in this chapter – just one part of the economy. A recent report from think tank, War on Want, documented how 101 mining companies listed on the London Stock Exchange control over $1 trillion worth of Africa's most valuable resources.[22] This is like Cecil Rhodes, but in the twenty first century – wealthy white owners in a world where the statement, 'the life of a black person in Africa is so cheap', remains horribly true. From race, to the environment, we need to understand what those at the top already know: capital is global.

It is not just capital that transcends borders. British lawyer James Nichol, who went to represent the families of the dead Marikana strikers in their quest for justice described feeling a sense of connection between their plight and his own upbringing in the coal mining town of North Walbottle, near Newcastle. He highlighted the common experience shared by so many across the world:

I've stood at the bottom of the street in a mining village and got a pan of hot food from a relative to take back to small children who were then living alone in the house. It can never be the same as a Marikana, but . . . I know they have no money, no food . . . Sentimental as I sound, that is why I came.[23]

---

22 Mark Curtis, *The New Colonialism: Britain's scramble for Africa's energy and mineral resources*, War on Want, report (2016) https://waronwant.org/sites/default/files/TheNewColonialism.pdf.

23 www.theguardian.com/world/2013/jan/06/marikana-mine-massacre-british-lawyer (last accessed 09/2019).

Chapter 2

Work: Less is more

We have all been there. You meet someone for the first time, introduce yourself and realise that you have absolutely nothing to talk about. As the conversation awkwardly starts to stall, one of you reaches for that question – 'So, what do you do for a living?'

Work is something we can all understand. Even if we have never had a job, we rely on the effort of others for everything we do: somebody worked to make and maintain the roads we walk on, the food we eat, the medicine we use, the cars we drive and, of course, the books we read. Work is all around us, yet we very rarely ask what it is and why we do it.

The phrase 'for a living' can shed some light on these questions. An inescapable and rather brutal fact about the world today is that in order to survive, you need money. Everything we need to live – food, clothes, water, shelter – comes with a price tag, and sometimes a big one. Ignoring for a moment the obvious exceptions (such as being born into highly unusual riches or winning the lottery) there is really only one way to make money: you have to sell something. Putting all your possessions on eBay might be one strategy, but this will only take you so far in rent and bills – besides, you need money to acquire those possessions in the first place. For most of us to survive in this world, there is one thing we have to sell – our time.

Work is an exchange: the worker sells their time (or as we often say 'spends their time') and gets a wage in return. Imagine for a moment that you have just been hired for a new job. After celebrating the good news, you will at some point be presented with a job contract – on the surface a rather boring document, but something that you should read very carefully, as it explains what you are signing up to. Written on the contract in black and white is the very essence of work – it will tell you the time you are giving up and the money you will receive in return.

Weekends

'Working 9–5 what a way to make a living'[1]

Selling time is not like selling an iPhone. In order for your time to be worth something to the person who has bought it, you actually have to do some work, and this requires effort and skills. Turning up to your job, sitting at your desk and doing literally nothing all day will probably get you fired. Work involves more than exchanging simply the hours of your day: it is about handing over control of your actions to your employer, who might regulate everything from how you should dress to where you need to sit.

Being told what to do is something we are all familiar with because we learn it from a very young age. Think about the commands of a normal school day, 'Do your tie! Sit down! Why haven't you done your homework?' Forget Maths and English – sitting in rows in front of an authority figure, following orders, being on time and looking presentable trains you for the world of work.

---

1 The song '9 to 5' by Dolly Parton was written about the workplace struggle of a group of female office workers in Boston fighting for fair pay and equal treatment.

The average British person spends eight hours a day from Monday to Friday at work. But who decided this? Unlike the 24-hour day which is determined by the rotation of the earth on its axis, there is nothing natural about the five day week and the two day weekend. In fact, until the nineteenth century, there was no concept of the weekend at all. Saturday was just another day, like Tuesday or Monday. In the smoky factories of the early Industrial Revolution, the average time spent at work was around double what it is now: a grinding 14–16 hour day, with only Sunday for rest (as instructed by the Bible).

We all know that feeling of a Monday morning, tucked up in bed and wanting nothing more than to turn off the alarm and fall back to sleep. Well 200 years ago people felt exactly the same, apart from one small difference. Unlike today, where we reluctantly manage to drag ourselves out of bed, these early factory workers did the opposite. Having a more rebellious spirit, they simply slept in and took the day off to chill. This tradition of not showing up for work on Monday became so widespread across the country it was even given its own name - 'Saint Monday' – mockingly named after an imaginary religious figure. Needless to say, this didn't go down well with the factory owners. As Saint Monday started to spread to Tuesday, panic also spread. Alongside social campaigners, such as Sir Ian McKellen's (best known for his role as Gandalf in Lord of the Rings) great, great grandfather, employers put forward the following deal to their employees: factories would close early on a Saturday without any reduction in wages so long as the tradition of Saint Monday was put to rest. In 1850, the first law along these lines was passed stopping work at exactly 2 p.m. on Saturday (which is incidentally why British football matches still kick off at 3 p.m.). Within a few years the pact had been made: Saint Monday was no more and the weekend was born. So next time you 'thank god it's Friday' make sure to pay your respect to those disobedient descendants and their Monday lie-ins.

Overwork

'It's enough to drive you crazy, if you let it.' [2]

The daily grind of the nine to five is just the average time spent on the job. In reality people work much more and much less than this. This raises the question – on average – are we working too much? It's a reasonable thing to ask in today's modern and hectic world – that is if we get the time to stop to think. Yet simply uttering this question is grounds for being dismissed as an entitled and sensitive snowflake, who has no understanding of a hard day's graft. This stereotype persists despite the fact that 16–25-year-olds, the supposedly lazy generation, actually work more overtime today than any other age group.[3] That said, the problem of overwork cuts across the whole workforce, with as much as one in four people in the UK working ten hours or more per week than they would like.[4]

Working too much puts serious pressure on people's physical health and mental well-being. According to the Health and Safety Executive, the government agency responsible for regulating workplace safety, the most common reason why people call in sick is not due to the flu or a bad hangover, but because of work-related stress and mental illness.[5] The demand to work less

2 Dolly Parton, '9 to 5'.

3 www.theguardian.com/careers/2015/oct/19/are-young-people-working-too-hard (last accessed 09/2019).

4 www.tuc.org.uk/research-analysis/reports/future-works-working-people (last accessed 09/2019).

5 Will Stronge and Aidan Harper, *The Shorter Working Week: A radical and pragmatic proposal* (Autonomy Research, 2019).

is not about laziness, but about our collective sanity. It is also a demand people have been calling for, ever since the idea of work (exchanging time for money) was invented.

Holiday

'There's a better life. And you think about it, don't you?'[6]

We all love going on holiday, but there is something even better than chilling on a beach – being paid to chill on the beach. Holiday pay is a legal right in the UK, but just because it's the law, it does not mean it is always properly enforced. One in twelve workers do not get their legally entitled holiday, and these tend to be in jobs primarily done by women and people of colour (an issue discussed further in the chapter nine on race).[7]

The situation in the UK is much better than in the United States, where businesses are not legally required to give their employees any paid leave. In 2015 the US government proposed changing the law so that all workers would get at least a measly five days paid holiday (in the UK the minimum for full time work is 28 days), but even this small demand was stopped by businesses who complained that it would increase unemployment.[8,9] In other words, the richest country in the world decided it couldn't afford to give its workers at least a week off; a right

---

6   Dolly Parton, '9 to 5'.

7   Nick Clark and Eva Herman, 'Unpaid Britain: wage default in the British labour market', Middlesex University, Report (2017) www.mdx.ac.uk/__data/assets/pdf_file/0017/440531/Final-Unpaid-Britain-report.pdf?bustCache=35242825 (last accessed 09/2019).

8   www.gov.uk/holiday-entitlement-rights (last accessed 09/2019).

9   www.bbc.com/worklife/article/20141106-the-no-vacation-nation (last accessed 09/2019).

that has existed in the UK since 1938, with no discernible effect on unemployment levels.

What happened in 1938 that couldn't be repeated in the US today? The 1930s in Britian was a rather tumultuous time. The country was on the brink of war with Nazi Germany and had just gone through a decade of economic downturn following the 1929 Great Depression. Only a very select and elite group of workers – supervisors and managers – had any paid holiday at all. For everyone else, holidays and festivals meant going without pay. Ultimately, the reason paid holiday was extended to most (but not all) workers in 1938 was because of a long campaign demanding it.

Starting in 1911, workers had been putting pressure on the government and businesses to change the law to give at least two weeks off a year. Central to the campaign, was the idea of the 'poor suffering British housewife'.[10] Holiday pay was sold to the British public on the grounds that it would give struggling housewives a break from their unpaid labour. A series of articles were published in the *Daily Herald* – a paper originally funded by the labour movement before turning into *The Sun* in 1964 – on how women could deal with cooking while away from home, under the headline 'Time Off for Mother'.

The recognition of unpaid labour as an important and valuable part of work was taken up by feminists at the time. In 1937 women organised a 'Seaside Campaign' around many of Britain's top tourist destinations throughout July and August. Distributing over 1 million leaflets and convening over 150 meetings, they argued for the universal right to paid leisure time. The campaign effectively targeted middle-class families while they were enjoying their time off. However, the focus on

---

10   Sandra Dawson, 'Working-Class Consumers and the Campaign for Holidays with Pay', *Twentieth Century British History* 18, no. 3, (2007): 277–305.

the British housewife also helped to reinforce the heteronorma-
tive and gendered stereotypes that we still see playing out today
– something we will discuss in greater detail in the next chapter.
The whole campaign reinforced the idea that the 'normal' family
ideal to aspire to, consists of a heterosexual couple, with the man
working outside the home for a wage, and a woman working in
the home without pay.

Even at the time, this ideal of the housewife and the male
breadwinner did not fit the realities playing out in the economy.
Women worked in both the home and the workplace, taking up
jobs ranging from industrial manual labour to cleaning. Many
women were also unmarried or ran single parent households,
with no male breadwinner in sight and in the face of rampant
sexist attitudes inside and outside the workplace. For example,
many trade unions at the time enforced a marriage bar, which
meant that a woman was effectively fired upon tying the knot.

By 1939, as the campaign built up strength, the government and businesses had started to come around to the idea of
paid holiday. They justified it in their own terms, arguing that
holiday pay would improve labour productivity and open new
business opportunities for the tourism industry. They eventually passed a law granting one paid week of holiday for millions
of workers. Looking back today, it was undoubtedly a victory.
But it did not go far enough. For starters, it fell short of the two
weeks demanded by the campaign. More importantly, despite
the act claiming that all workers should have the right to paid
holiday, the way it defined who counted as a worker was narrow,
gendered and exclusionary. Part-time and domestic service
workers, which was generally seen as women's work, were not
covered by the act, and therefore were not considered in the eyes
of those who implemented it to be true workers. This inequality
was undoubtedly in part due to the gendered stereotypes perpet-

uated by the campaign, which diminished women's actual role in the workplace to uphold the ideal of the housewife.

Precarious work

'Barely getting' by. It's all takin' and no giving' [11]

So far, we have discussed the problem of working too much and the demand to work less for the same pay – two issues that are intricately related. But lately an issue at work that deals with almost the opposite problem has become a worry across the world. That is the problem of not working enough. The problem of precarious work.

Precarious work is, to a large extent, about the vulnerability of time: having little security over the time you spend at work. Nothing embodies this vulnerability like the zero-hour contract. Let's go back to that job contract we started with and imagine flicking through the pages and stumbling across the number of hours worked. A zero-hour contract is when there are no guaranteed hours. You have a job under your belt, but the hours worked week-by-week need to be agreed with your employer. These types of contracts have risen astronomically in recent years – there were over 400 per cent more people on them in 2017 than in 2002 – and are currently used across the economy, from Domino's Pizza to Buckingham Palace. [12]

Zero-hour contracts are often depicted by employers as empowering for workers, opening up the freedom to work as they wish, outside of the shackles of the monotonous nine-

---

11 Dolly Parton, '9 to 5'.

12 www.ons.gov.uk/employmentandlabourmarket/peopleinwork/employmentand employeetypes/bulletins/uklabourmarket/september2017 (last accessed 09/2019).

to-five daily grind. 'Fancy working today? Great! Fancy doing something else? Also great!'

Yet the reality of these contracts is just the opposite of this. The power to turn work on and off like a tap sits almost exclusively with the employer. A zero-hour contract means you work when your boss wants you to work. So often this means not working enough, with people on zero-hour contracts being over three times more likely to want more hours than a regular worker.[13] And if you ever decide to cancel a shift to spend a sunny day in the park you will be punished accordingly, as over a third of all people on zero-hour contracts have been threatened with losing future shifts if they turn down work.

Those who defend the use of these contracts also argue that zero-hour contracts are just a marginal issue, that the real problem is not whether people are on precarious contracts, but whether they have a job in the first place. In other words, they argue that precarious work does not really matter so long as the rate of unemployment – the proportion of people who want a job but cannot find one – is kept down. These days it is common to turn on the TV and hear pundits, economists and politicians all arguing that unemployment figures in the UK are at record low levels, and that zero-hour contracts are ultimately great for the average Joe. Yet focusing on the unemployment figures ignores the fact that many of the new jobs do not provide enough hours or high enough wages for people to live, feed and look after themselves. Statistically, more people in the UK now suffer from underwork than unemployment. In 2014, for the first time since records began, there were more people who wanted more hours in their current job, than people who were unemployed.[14]

---

13 www.theguardian.com/uk-news/2018/apr/23/number-of-zero-hours-contracts-in-uk-rose-by-100000-in-2017-ons (last accessed 09/2019).

14 ONS, *UK labour market: September 2017* (Labour Force Survey, 2017).

A recent report showed that one in six workers in the UK (5.1 million people) are in low paid insecure work. That's a huge chunk of the population who are working unpredictable hours; on an agency, casual, seasonal or fixed term contract but want to be a permanent employee; or self-employed and earning less than the living wage.[15]

That so many workers are currently employed under precarious conditions explains why simply getting a job is not enough to bring people out of poverty. Despite unemployment in 2019 being at a record low, in-work poverty is at the highest it has been in 20 years.[16] Over half (58 per cent) of those who live in poverty come from a working household, compared to just 37 per cent in the 1990s.[17] If getting a job is fundamentally about making a living, then something has clearly gone wrong: work is not working.

Working until you die

'It's a rich man's game, No matter what they call it, And you spend your life, Putting money in his wallet.'[18]

There is a quote by billionaire Warren Buffett, who we will look at more in Chapter 4, which summarises how the economy splits people into classes. According to him, we live in a system where, 'either you make money while you sleep or you work till you die'.

15   Katherine Chapman and Stuart Wright, *Living Hours Report* (Living Wage Foundation, 2019).

16   Helen Barnard, *UK Poverty 2018*, (The JRF Analysis Unit, The Joseph Roundtree Foundation, 2018) www.jrf.org.uk/report/uk-poverty-2018.

17   Pascale Bourquin, Jonathan Cribb, Tom Waters and Xiaowei Xu, *Living standards, poverty and inequality in the UK: 2019* (The Institute for Fiscal Studies, Report, 2019).

18   Dolly Parton, '9 to 5'.

It is often said that the most common thing people wish for on their deathbed is to have spent less time in the office. While we are young and alive we must remember that we can grant this wish, so long as we demand it collectively. As we have seen throughout this chapter, people have always fought back against work taking over their lives. We have only looked at two cases: holidays and weekends. But there are many more – the eight hour day, retirement age, the average wage, pensions, sick pay, taxation, the right to unionise, unemployment benefits, health-care. All these things that shape how much we work is the result of the balance of class power in the economy, between those that sell their time and those that make money while they sleep; between labour and capital.

This balance of power currently stands at a knife-edge. If it is tipped in favour of capital, we are likely to go down the road of more and more work; faster and faster days; and the extension of the retirement age to 75, which the UK government at the time of writing has proposed – higher than the life expectancy for men in the most deprived areas of the UK.[19] If we tip it in favour of labour, there is the potential to work less, best encapsulated in the demand for a four-day working week – a continuation of the struggle for leisure time that started with those Monday lie-ins so long ago.

All this raises the question – who is the 'we' that is included in 'labour'? The working class, as the name suggests, are the people that need to work in order to live. This is undeniably a very broad and blunt definition of class. In some respects this breadth is a positive thing, as it allows us to see class as a force at the heart of the modern economy, rather than an outdated idea that only

19 www.ons.gov.uk/peoplepopulationandcommunity/healthandsocialcare/health inequalities/bulletins/healthstatelifeexpectanciesbyindexofmultipledeprivation imd/2015to2017 (last accessed 09/2019).

makes sense when dressed in flat caps and overalls. Picking up the phones in a call centre, looking after people in a care home, stacking shelves in a supermarket, teaching a chemistry class, sitting at a hotel reception, delivering food – the working class in Britain today is a broad, diverse, multi-ethnic, and mostly unorganised mass of people. The power of labour to demand a better life from capital will depend on how collectively organised this group is. With that said, understanding class along such broad lines should not paint over the deep inequalities that exist within what we call 'labour'. There are many privileged well-paid middle-class people that still need to earn a wage in order to survive, but are vastly better off than the poor. There are also the deep divisions along gender, race, sexuality and ability that shape divisions in the world. It is to the former of these inequalities – gender – to which we now turn.

Chapter 3

Gender: Please mind the gap

When it comes to the news, the BBC sits at the heart of the British media establishment. In between reporting on the latest political crisis, the BBC will occasionally get caught up in its own media scandal, with the summer of 2017 being one of those moments where the cameras and commentators turned in on themselves. Following the publication of the salaries of all employees at the corporation, the BBC had inadvertently showed the world that it had a serious gender pay gap problem.

Most of the coverage focused on the pay gap between the rich celebrities at the top of the BBC. The released documents showed that of the best paid presenters, the top seven were all men. DJ and former host of *Top Gear*, Chris Evans, topped the list, having made a whopping £2.25m that year – five times the salary of the top female star, *Strictly Come Dancing* lead, Claudia Winkelman.

The gender pay gap is not solely an issue at the BBC – it permeates practically every economic institution in society. Statistically speaking, the gender pay gap measures the differences in the salaries of the average (median) worker. Suppose you lined up in two lines, all the male workers and all the female workers in the country from the best to the worst paid. The gender pay gap is simply the difference in the wages of the two people in the middle of each line. In the UK, this difference is 20 per cent, which means for every £1 that the middle worker in the male line earns, the middle female worker earns just 80 pence.[1]

Like the BBC case, discussions of the gender pay gap tend to focus on the gap between rich men and rich women. Whether it's Hollywood actors or CEO managers, the debate often looks solely at the gendered differences within the elite classes, rather than the difference between say rich men and poor women. Analysing the gendered inequality of the richest in our society does give us a sense of how pervasive gendered stereotypes actually are. For example, a recent study assessing why women were under-represented in the top professions found that in general, men were seen as 'rational and decisive' – valued leadership traits – while women were seen as emotional, well-organised and ethical.[2] But questioning why one group of millionaires (rich women) are less wealthy than another group of millionaires (rich men) does not seem relevant to most women's lives. Very few people will ever become a CEO of a multinational corporation, or a famous BBC presenter. As journalist Dawn Foster explains, 'For decades, the measure of success for the feminist movement in some quarters has simply been how many women are present at the very top, regardless of what happens to the bulk of women at the very bottom of society.'[3] It's time then to refocus the analysis.

What causes the gender pay gap? In answering this question we need to stop looking at the inequalities within the elite and

---

1   Monica Costa Dias, Robert Joyce and Francesca Parodi, *The gender pay gap in the UK: children and experience in work* (The Institute of Fiscal Studies, working paper, 2018).

2   Dawn Foster, *Lean Out* (Repeater, 2016), pp. 1-87.

3   Ibid.

think about how the whole economy and class system that support it are structured along patriarchal lines.

The gender pay gap is often confused with a related but connected issue: unequal pay for the same job. The difference between Claudia Winkelman and Chris Evans above is a clear example of unequal pay. It's quite hard to make an argument that the presenter of *Top Gear* is worth five times the presenter of *Strictly Come Dancing*, particularly given the fact that the car show's ratings crashed and burned after Chris Evans took control of the wheel. They are doing similar work, but being paid radically different amounts. Such inequality can arise from a range of sources, from outright gendered discrimination by employers to internalised gendered attitudes that workers have regarding asking for pay rises. And while the evidence on how much pay gaps are the result of unequal pay is divided, what is clear is that even if we made sure that everyone were paid equally for the same job, there would still be a sizeable gender pay gap.[4] Something else is going on.

Occupational segregation: The hidden figures

We live in an economic system where jobs are divided between genders. Some work is seen as a man's job, while others are assumed to be done by women. Alongside Adam Smith's famous division of labour (which you can read about on the back of every £20 note) our economy also has a gendered division of labour,

---

4   Evidence that unequal pay does matter for pay gaps: www.ons.gov.uk/
employmentandlabourmarket/peopleinwork/earningsandworkinghours/articles/
understandingthegenderpaygapintheuk/2018-01-17 (last accessed 09/2019).

Evidence that it is less important: Benjamin Frost, Peggy Hazard, Dési Kimmins, *The real gap: fixing the gender pay divide* (Korn Ferry, report, 2016).

whether it's lawyers versus secretaries; doctors versus nurses; managers versus cashiers or computer scientists versus carers.

Where does the 'occupational segregation' come from? In short, it is upheld by the type of gendered stereotypes we saw above, which assume that men tend to be cool-headed, rational and strong leaders, while women are stereotyped as emotional, caring followers. We learn these norms from a young age and they are reinforced through the media, jokes, career advisors, books and films. So, jobs which require leadership qualities or rely on intellect become dominated by men, whereas those professions that are linked to the home – such as care work and cleaning – or those jobs that have a more supportive role – like secretaries, teaching, nursing – are traditionally feminised. In the UK alone, just over three quarters of working women in the UK are employed in one of the 'fives Cs' – care, clerical (administrative), cashiering (retail), catering and cleaning.[5]

If these feminised jobs were paid roughly the same as male jobs, then occupational segregation would not lead to pay gaps. In the real world though, jobs that are traditionally seen as women's work are paid less on average than male professions.[6] This brings us to a fundamental question about work and class. Why are some jobs paid more than others? In mainstream economics, we are told that pay reflects how productive a person is: the more skilled, educated, experienced and profitable they are, the more they will be rewarded. This narrative conveniently ignores the fact that wages also reflect social and political power

5   D. Kamerade and H. Richardson, *Gender segregation, underemployment and subjective wellbeing in the UK labour market* (University of Salford, 2017). This version is available at: http://usir.salford.ac.uk/id/eprint/42283.
6   Wendy Olsen, Vanessa Gash, Sook Kim, Min Zhang, *The gender pay gap in the UK: evidence from the UKHLS* (Government and Equalities Office, Social Sciences in Government, Research Report, May 2018).

relations. In our patriarchal society, women's work is paid less not because it requires less skills or contributes less to overall economic activity. It is valued less *because* it is seen as women's work.

To see this point clearly, let us look at an example of a profession which has, over the course of history, changed gender. In the words of James Brown, the tech industry today is 'a man's world', with women making up only 26 per cent of computer and mathematical jobs in the US.[7] And while there is certainly exploitation in the industry,[8] programmers enjoy a prestige and pay packet above say a cleaner or care worker. But this has not always been the case. In the past, computer programming was seen as women's work, as captured in the 2017 film *Hidden Figures*, based on the true story of three black women working at NASA during the Apollo missions. The film starts with the Soviet Union launch of Sputnik in 1957 – the first artificial satellite in space. Soviet technology precipitated a major crisis in the West. When John F. Kennedy became President in 1961, he told Congress that by the end of the decade, the US would achieve the impossible, 'landing a man on the Moon and returning him safely to the Earth.' But for the first few years, the US lagged behind in the space race, with the Soviets putting the first man in space in April 1961 and the first women in space in 1963 – something the US would not achieve for another 20 years.

Hidden Figures follows the forgotten history of the black female programmers and mathematicians that built the Apollo space programme. From performing calculations to programming early computers, these women did the majority of the

---

7   www.nytimes.com/2019/02/13/magazine/women-coding-computer-programming.html (last accessed 09/2019).

8   Jamie Woodcock, *Marx at the Arcade* (Haymarket Books, London, 2019).

intellectual heavy lifting – so much so that they were literally called 'computers'. But the fact that these 'computers' were both *black* and *female* meant that their work, despite being incredibly intellectual, complicated and challenging, was devalued as low skilled, monotonous and clerical.

There is not just one way to 'be a woman'. Being a trans woman or a black woman means your experience of womanhood is clearly very different to that of a white, cis-woman. For instance, women of colour in the UK today face far more economic inequality than white women, they have had to shoulder more of the burden of welfare cuts, and after graduating from university, will make less money than a white woman without a university degree at all.[9] Much like today, being a black woman in 1960s Alabama meant being confronted with both racism and sexism. As the film shows, NASA's offices at the time were racially segregated, with women of colour unable to use the same toilets as the white female workers.

Over time, as computer technology advanced and its role in our lives became more and more important, men started to take over the field. In one study that looked at why men started to dominate computer programming throughout the 1980s, the researchers found that the rise of men in the profession came with the rise of the personal computer. Parents were much more likely to buy personal computers for their sons rather than their daughters, which meant boys got a head start in the field before studying at university. The idea quickly spread that computers were for boys.[10]

---

9   Sarah-Marie Hall et al., *Intersecting inequalities: The impact of austerity on Black and Minority Ethnic women in the UK*, (Women's Budget Group, Runnymede Trust, Coventry Women's Voices, RECLAIM, 2017).

10   Allan Fisher and Jane Margolis, *Unlocking the Clubhouse: Women in Computing* (The MIT Press, 2002).

If we are to draw a radical message from *Hidden Figures* it would be this: the most groundbreaking and important work can easily be forgotten and undervalued. Just like cleaning, nursing and teaching today, some of the most important jobs that keep our society functioning, are desperately underpaid. While some might argue that bankers, academics and CEOs are paid more because they contribute more to the economy, we need to remember that pay is as much about power as it is about productivity. Imagine for a moment what would happen if all the hedge fund managers in The City of London decided to collectively quit their jobs. How much of an impact on our lives would this actually have? While I am sure there is a case to be argued that the loss of these jobs would cause some damage to the economy, it is not unreasonable to ask whether the world might actually be a better place? Compare this to an alternative case where all the paid carers – the workers who look after children, the elderly and the sick – stopped turning up for work. The negative human impact would be undeniably immediate and devastating.

Unpaid work: Toil and trouble

The gender pay gap does not just reflect what happens in the workplace. At the beginning of the last chapter we asked: 'how do most people survive when they grow up?' While we concluded that they have to sell their time for a wage, this presupposes the question – who looks after you before you can, both literally and metaphorically, stand on your own two feet? Think about how many dishes have been cleaned, how many clothes have been washed, how many floors have been swept, how many shopping trips have been done, how many school pickups have been organised, to get you to where you are today. Across most of the world, the person most likely to do all these jobs will be a woman, and they are likely to be doing it for free.

All this unpaid domestic work has a huge impact on the gender pay gap. On average, having children has a massive negative impact on the wages of women, but when men have children it barely makes a dent. This is not because having a child suddenly makes women worse at their jobs. The reason is largely due to the fact that women are the ones who have to take time off or go down to part-time work due to childcare duties.[11] As touched on in the last chapter around paid holiday, the idea that women are solely responsible for doing housework has been circulating for a long time. The idea that a man's place is in the office and a woman's place is in the home goes back to the beginning of waged work itself: to the very origins of capitalism.

Although people in modern society find it difficult to imagine an alternative to capitalism, it's an economic system which has not always existed. Capitalism has a beginning and an end, just like the Roman Empire. Before it came about, Britain had a feudal economic system where the vast majority of people were peasants. To be a peasant meant to live off the land – a plot to farm, communal water to drink, and forests to forage for wood. They were not rich, but they had the basic things they needed to survive – food, water, shelter and community. This 'right of habitation' was enshrined in a long tradition of English law going back centuries to the 1217 Charter of the Forest.[12] But by the fifteenth century things began to change. The Feudal lords – the land-owning nobility – slowly began to realise that they could increase their wealth by privatising the common land. Peasants were kicked off the land, fences and hedges were put up and large

---

11 www.ifs.org.uk/publications/10356.
12 Jason Hickel, *The Divide: A Brief Guide to Global Inequality and its Solutions* (William Heinemann, 2017).

farms and sheep pastures were created. The nobility employed the most productive and hardworking peasants to work these farms, increasing production and wealth for the landowners. The rest of the peasantry had to fend for themselves – an unenviable task, given that they no longer had access to the woods, rivers and land necessary for survival.

This radical transformation has a name – the *enclosure* of the common land – and it is where the seeds of our class system today were born, creating the first labour market and a group of disposed people who needed to earn a wage to survive. As we saw in Chapter 1, in South Africa, the enclosure of common lands would be repeated across the colonies in the building of the global capitalist system. But this was not the only 'great transformation' occurring.[13] Throughout the same period, hundreds of thousands of women across Europe were being hunted down, tortured and burned in the organised persecution we now call the witch hunt. According to academic and activist Silvia Federici, the witchhunts were a crucial step in trying to lock women in the home. Under feudalism women worked on the land, co-producing the wealth for the commons. With the witch hunts this all started to change. Women, who had once worked the land with men, were starting to be stigmatised if they joined them in the fields, and women's public voices were silenced under the climate of fear, suspicion and terror of the hunts.

The church and the state set about on a 'war against women' in a bid to control them.[14] In particular there was a focus on controlling women's reproductive capacity and enforcing the idea that a woman's place was in the home where she would raise the new labour force. While there is obviously no such thing as

---

13   Karl Polanyi, *The Great Transformation* (1944).
14   Silvia Federici, *Caliban and the Witch Women, The Body And Primitive Accumulation* (Autonomedia, 2014).

an actual witch, and the women who were burned came from all classes and backgrounds, many of them were involved in alternative medicine, in particular using natural remedies for menstrual and hormonal problems, performing abortions and administering contraceptives. Others were targeted because they were single, adulterous, lesbians or simply not interested in procreating. In short, most of those who were killed were in some way rejecting the expectation that a woman should be in a marriage, in the home and giving birth to children.

Over the centuries these stereotypes of what a woman should be has been reinforced and refined, and despite strong resistance from feminist movements across the world, still lives on to this day. As Silvia Federici concludes, 'Not only has housework been imposed on women, but it has been transformed into a natural attribute of our female physique and personality, an internal need, an aspiration, supposedly coming from the depth of our female character.'[15] We see this so clearly today in the unequal distribution of who does this work. Over 74 per cent of time spent looking after children in the UK is done by women, and women spend 26 hours per week on average doing unpaid domestic work[16] – nearly double the amount done by men each week.[17] The history of women and capitalism is quite literally one of 'double, double toil and trouble'.

The gender pay gap has a long history and the demand for equal pay gets to the very core of the class system. So far in the book we have only looked at the capital-labour relation and the world

---

15   Silvia Federici, *Wages Against Housework* (Falling Wall Press Ltd, 1975).

16   Will Stronge and Aidan Harper, *The Shorter Working Week: A radical and pragmatic proposal* (Autonomy, Autonomy Research, 2019).

17   www.ons.gov.uk/employmentandlabourmarket/peopleinwork/earningsand
workinghours/articles/womenshouldertheresponsibilityofunpaidwork/2016-11-10,
(last accessed 09/2019).

of work. To this we must add the way that women's work, both inside and outside the home, has historically been undervalued. This is despite the fact that much of this work is the bedrock that enables the economy to function. Because all of this labour plays a central part in the story of capitalism, we need to remember that you don't need to be working for a wage to be part of the working class. The writer Reni Eddo-Lodge argues in her book *Why I'm No Longer Talking to White People About Race*, 'We should be rethinking the image we conjure up when we think of a working-class person. Instead of a white man in a flat cap, it's a black woman pushing a pram.'[18] More than oil, data, or money, the unpaid care work of mothers pushing prams creates the fundamental component that no economy can live without: people. Tackling the gender pay gap is therefore a much more structural problem than simply issuing quotas or transparency over pay. To really challenge the gap, we need to tackle the constant undervaluing of women's work and the gendered stereotypes that have allowed this to persist throughout the generations.

---

18 Reni Eddo-Lodge, *Why I'm No Longer Talking to White People About Race* (Bloomsbury Publishing, London, 2017).

Chapter 4

Money: Who wants to be a billionaire?

Mark Zuckerberg, Bill Gates, Jeff Bezos, Kylie Jenner, Elon Musk, Trump – these billionaire celebrities are some of the most recognisable names in the world. Their wealth brings them fame, and their fame brings them wealth, vindicating what the economist Adam Smith could see as far back as 1759: 'The rich man glories in his riches, because he feels that they naturally draw upon him the attention of the world'.[1] Today the wealthy don't just catch our attention; they draw our admiration. From mainstream economists to politicians, we have been told that the wealthiest in society are at the top because they deserve to be there. Through hard work, intelligence and creative thinking, they have built companies and innovative products that billions throughout the world need, want and desire. Whether it's keeping up with friends thanks to Zuckerberg's Facebook or using Bezos' Amazon to shop without getting out of bed, we are told that the wealthier they get, the wealthier we become. As the phrase goes: a rising tide lifts all boats.

There are 2,153 billionaires in the world. Their combined wealth is $8.6 trillion.[2] The above argument might suggest that

---

1 Adam Smith, *The Theory of Moral Sentiments* (Kessinger Publishing, 2010).
2 www.forbes.com/sites/willyakowicz/2019/03/09/how-the-worlds-billionaires-got-so-rich/#7d8b42f6ae6e (last accessed 09/2019).

they deserve their wealth, that more money at the top means more money for the rest of us. But is this true? To answer this, we will take a look at some of the richest people on this planet to uncover where such astronomical wealth comes from – and what their fortunes mean for everyone else.

The rich kids

Let's start with some of the worst, most egregious examples – the billionaires who have made it onto the list via a bloody mix of violence, theft and illegal expropriation. One of these is the man who made billions running the diamond trade in the Democratic Republic of Congo during its civil war, Dan Gertler. Over 5 million people have died in the conflict; it is the deadliest the world has seen since the Second World War. Gertler's commercial endeavors cost the country more than $1.3 billion in just three years, with the UN referring to his monopoly as a 'nightmare'. Curiously enough, $1.3 billion is almost exactly the amount Dan Gertler has stashed away in his private fortune. It's also double the figure that the DRC (a country with 81.34 million of the poorest people in the world) spends on health and education each year.[3]

Another shady character on the billionaires list is Joaquin 'El Chapo' Guzman Loera, the infamous Mexican Drug Lord of the Sinaloa Cartel. Having escaped prison twice, at the time of writing he's standing trial in the US where he has been accused of an unbelievable list of crimes including: paying off the President of Mexico for $100 million; burying his enemies alive; killing a man and his wife for failing to shake his hand; and delivering in

---

3 www.globalwitness.org/en/blog/gertler-received-and-distributed-millions-bribes-connection-drc-mining-deals-court-papers-allege (last accessed 09/2019).

just four shipments, 328 million lines of cocaine – the equivalent of a line for every single American citizen.[4]

There are also those billionaires who were simply born rich. Not that they would all like to admit their fortunes are just that – fortunate. Gina Rinehart, an Australian billionaire who inherited a mining dynasty, came under controversy when she said that 'if you're jealous of those with more money, don't just sit there and complain. Do something to make more money yourself – spend less time drinking or smoking and socializing, and more time working.'[5] Many felt it was ironic that a woman who makes $600 a second could also claim that Australians should be 'willing to work for less than $2 a day'.

Then there are the billionaires who are most famous for their lavish, opulent lifestyles. Indian oil magnate Mukesh Ambani tops the list for the most over the top luxury purchase ever, having built a $1 billion mansion in Mumbai with 27 floors, 3 helicopter pads and 600 members of staff. This is in a city where 42 per cent of the population lives in slums.

The long list of 2,153 billionaires is littered with these Bond villains. They are what we might call the illegitimate face of capitalism. In some cases, their activities are illegal, while in others they display grotesque greed that even the most ardent supporter of the capitalist economy will find it hard to defend such fortunes. But what about the wealthy who are considered the 'legitimate' face of capitalism? Let's take a look at the do-gooders who are seen to benefit the rest of the world.

---

4   www.bbc.co.uk/news/world-us-canada-46282173 (last accessed 09/2019).
5   www.npr.org/sections/thetwo-way/2012/09/05/160614909/asias-richest-woman-slammed-after-musing-about-workers-paid-2-a-day?t=1562602296282 (last accessed 09/2019).

The good guys

When it comes to 'good' capitalists, there is one person who tops the list. Warren Buffett is the third richest person in the world, with a total wealth of over $80 billion. Despite accumulating a vast fortune, he still lives in the same house that he did in the 1950s. His offices are not in a glittering New York skyscraper, but in Omaha, Nebraska, a small city with a population of less than half a million people. His catchy phrases (remember 'make money while you sleep or work till you die') and humility has even earned him the nickname as the 'Oracle of Omaha'. Buffett has argued that the richest in American society should pay much higher taxes than they currently do. He recently complained that in the US, the tax laws are so unfair that as a billionaire he actually pays a lower proportional tax rate than his cleaner. But his most benevolent act by far has been his pledge to give away 99 per cent of his fortune to charity, while urging other rich people across the world to follow suit. Buffett is not all talk: since 2000 he has given away more than $46 billion,[6] making him one of the most generous philanthropists in the history of humanity.

Buffett made his money in the way most billionaires do these days – as a financial investor.[7] His method is relatively simple: he finds companies he thinks will do well and buys their stock. Bankers and investors generally have a bad reputation due to the reckless financial speculation that led to the global financial crisis in 2008 (an issue to be discussed further in Chapter 7). Buffett, however, rejects this kind of recklessness. Four years before the crisis, he predicted that the big banks were running a

6   www.cnbc.com/2017/09/21/warren-buffet-is-the-most-charitable-billionaire. html (last accessed 09/2019).
7   https://www.forbes.com/sites/willyakowicz/2019/03/09/how-the-worlds-billionaires-got-so-rich.

risky business building complex financial instruments, which he called 'financial weapons of mass destruction'.[8] When the crisis did eventually hit, big investment banks like Goldman Sachs turned to Buffett for a bailout.

Buffett looks clean. But in order to understand where his money comes from, we need to look at the companies he owns and how they make their profits. Over the years he has invested in hundreds of companies, but there is one in particular that has been his prize investment: Coca-Cola. Since 1988, when he first put $1 billion into the fizzy drinks company, he has been its largest shareholder.[9] As he told Coca-Cola's shareholders in 2019, 'We have never sold a share and I would never think of selling a share',[10] before cracking open a can of the cold stuff (he claims to drink four cans of Coke a day.)

Coca-Cola is everywhere. There are only two countries in the world where the company's drinks are not formally sold – Cuba and North Korea – and even there it is easy to get hold of on the black market. Coca-Cola is one of the most recognisable brands on the planet, which is unsurprising given that it spends roughly $4 billion a year on advertising.[11] A third of all the beverages (other than water) consumed around the world are owned by Coca-Cola. That's 1.9 billion servings of Coca-Cola owned drinks each day.

Coca-Cola is so ubiquitous that we probably don't stop to think how it gets to our fridges. But a quick look at its history since Warren Buffett became the major shareholder shows us that the company is not as sweet as it tastes.

---

8   http://news.bbc.co.uk/1/hi/2817995.stm (last accessed 09/2019).

9   www.coca-colacompany.com/stories/i-like-to-bet-on-sure-things-warren-buffett-on-why-hell-never-sell-a-share-of-coke-stock (last accessed 09/2019).

10   Ibid.

11   www.investopedia.com/articles/markets/081315/look-cocacolas-advertising-expenses.asp (last accessed 09/2019).

Killer Coke

Across the world Coca-Cola is infamous for trampling on workers' rights. Its most notorious scandal occurred eight years after Buffett got involved. On 5 December 1996, in the town of Carepa in the North West of Colombia, two people on a motorbike skidded past the doorway of a local Coca-Cola bottling plant, looking for Isidro Gil, the president of the local union. When they found him standing in the doorway, they pulled out their guns and fired, killing him instantly. It was the first casualty in a series of coordinated attacks by paramilitary groups on Coca-Cola bottlers that day. Within a few hours, they had burned down the union offices and forced any remaining members to flee.

Colombia at the time was in the midst of a long spell of political violence, which ultimately killed 28,000 people and displaced over 2 million people from their homes. During the turmoil, anyone trying to organise in their workplace was specially targeted by right-wing paramilitary groups.[12] In the lead up to his death, Isidro Gil had been leading the fight for higher wages, job protections and safety from these very groups (it is reported that one local paramilitary organisation had played football with someone's head just days before the shooting).[13] After Gil's assassination, wages in the bottling plant were slashed in half.[14]

Coca-Cola rarely pulls out of a country because of politics. During the Second World War, Coca-Cola plants in Nazi

---

12 Over 4,000 union members were assassinated between 1986 and 2003. See Gill (2007) below.

13 www.theatlantic.com/health/archive/2010/10/the-pause-that-represses-coca-colas-controversies/64456 (last accessed 09/2019).

14 L. Gill, 'Right There with You': Coca-Cola, Labor Restructuring and Political Violence in Colombia', *Critique of Anthropology* 27, no. 3, (2007): 235–60.

Germany could not import the US manufactured syrups due to a trade embargo. Rather than leaving the Third Reich, the company decided to experiment with ingredients they could find locally. They put together a mix of apple and sugar and named it after the German word for 'imagination' to celebrate their quick thinking – Fanta.

Back in Colombia, the members of the union who had escaped the coordinated attack that had killed Isidro decided to fight back against Coca-Cola. In 2001, they filed a lawsuit against the company, accusing it of collusion. Two years later they launched a global campaign to expose what had happened, attacking Coca-Cola's most valuable asset – its brand. Alongside protesting outside the company's headquarters in Atlanta, they organised a successful boycott of Coke products in 16 universities in the US, and many more across the world.

While it's fair to say that Coca-Cola doesn't make its billions from murdering its employees every day, the way the company defended its reputation inside and outside the courtroom highlighted how 'the real thing' really makes it profits. Coca-Cola has consistently denied responsibility for the murders, hiding behind the fact that it technically did not own the bottling plants in Colombia. Like almost all multinational corporations, Coca-Cola organises its global supply chains so as to outsource as much of its dirty work as possible to someone else. We might call it the 'it's not my business' way of doing business. Put simply, Coke doesn't own its bottlers, or its sugar plantations, just like Apple doesn't own its iPhone factories. This allows these brands to be kept at arm's length from the messy, dangerous and degrading work that goes into producing their products day in and day out, creating a veneer of innocence and ignorance in case anything is ever demanded of them. Outsourcing has created the perfect excuse to ignore the demands and rights of anyone who might get in the way of profits.

Over 20 years on from the murder of Isidro Gil, we see this today in almost every corner of the globe: in Ireland Coca-Cola has refused to recognise the bottlers union and have threatened to close the plant if their workers organise; in Indonesia union leaders have been fired and members have been harassed following a 20-year long campaign to get recognition;[15] in Haiti four union leaders and over 100 workers have been dismissed after complaining that workers had not been paid the minimum wage, which in Haiti is only $5–7 a day;[16] in the Philippines workers have been laid off *en masse* and replaced with lower wages and more precarious conditions;[17] and in Colombia, as the country moves on from its violent past, Coca-Cola has opened up a new mega plant, firing some of the workforce and replacing secure work with precarious contracts.[18]

Tax haven treasure islands

Outsourcing is not the only way Coca-Cola makes profits. It has also built a system where it offloads as much of its costs onto somebody else – the taxpayer. Ever since its inception in 1892, Coca-Cola has let local governments pay for the water and recycling systems that are needed to distribute and sell the product.[19] This wouldn't necessarily be a problem if Coca-Cola paid back what it took in the form of taxes. But like so many

15   www.iuf.org/w/?q=node/5794 (last accessed 09/2019).

16   www.fairlabor.org/tr/node/2161 (last accessed 09/2019).

17   www.iuf.org/ccww/?q=node/798 (last accessed 09/2019).

18   https://witnessforpeace.org/coca-colas-new-bottling-plant-threatens-workers-rights-in-colombia (last accessed 09/2019).

19   https://fortune.com/2014/11/25/coca-cola-capitalism (last accessed 09/2019).

companies, Coca-Cola participates in a global system of tax avoidance, hiding billions in tax havens – the treasure islands of today's financial economy.

The way most companies avoid tax is surprisingly simple. Coca-Cola's headquarters are in the US, but it has many branches of the company in countries across the world – what are called subsidiaries. When Coca-Cola UK imports sugary syrups from Coca-Cola US, it pays a price for the products and actually transfers money to the US branch. The money stays within the Coca-Cola company but it moves from the UK to the US. This is known as transfer pricing and it is a common and legal part of the global economy. In fact, most global trade, 60%, is conducted within companies rather than between them.

Transfer pricing becomes a problem when it is used to game the tax system. Suppose the Coca-Cola company in the US wants to shift money to a tax haven like the Cayman Islands. Rather than charging a normal price for syrups, the subsidiary in the Cayman Islands increases and therefore manipulates the price it charges for its services, in order for money to flow into the tax haven. From the view of the tax authorities, it just looks like a normal internal trade. In reality it is a disguise for illicit flows on a vast scale. This is known as transfer mispricing and it is exactly what Coca-Cola has been doing since the 1980s. According to one report, it has accumulated a vast treasure trove of nearly $33.3 billion in various tax havens, leading to the loss of billions in revenue for governments across the world.[20]

For Coca-Cola executives sitting in its head office in Atlanta there is only one reason why they avoid tax, weaken labour regulation, outsource production, fire workers, and pay them below the minimum wage: to maximise the shareholder value of their

20 www.oxfamamerica.org/static/media/files/Broken_at_the_Top_FINAL_EMBARGOED_4.12.2016.pdf (last accessed 09/2019).

company. The CEO of Coca-Cola during the 80s and 90s put it most clearly when he said: 'I wrestle over how to build shareholder value from the time I get up in the morning to the time I go to bed. I even think about it when I am shaving.'[21]

Does a rising tide lift all boats?

How do the wealthy get rich? Rather than looking at the Dr Evils of the billionaire list, we have focused on the story behind Warren Buffett – the respectable and legitimate face of the capitalist class – to try and answer this question. By his own words, Warren Buffett is 'a card-carrying capitalist'. He embodies many of the stereotypical features of his class: the constant need to continue accumulating (he is nearly 90 but continues to run the company), a fortune built from scratch, an ability to sniff out a profitable investment and a philanthropic moral code. In short, he is a capitalist who plays by the rules of capitalism.

Yet what Buffett's fortune exposes is that these rules do not work in everyone's interests. The class system, even with its most respectable face on, is one where the wealth of the richest relies on a system that keeps the poor in their place. His fortune is kept afloat by the profits of Coca-Cola, which are extracted by avoiding tax, outsourcing production and undermining the rights and pay of its employees. Coca-Cola is by no means the worst offender. Almost every corporation listed on the world's stock exchanges makes profits this way. It is the economic system working as it's supposed to.

You might be thinking that – despite the damage done by Coca-Cola – is it not the case that Buffett has redeemed himself

---

21   www.theatlantic.com/health/archive/2010/10/the-pause-that-represses-coca-colas-controversies/64456.

with the vast fortune he has given away to charity? Surely the benefits outweigh the costs?

This is Buffett's own view. He told the New York Times in 2019, 'nothing rivals the market system in producing what people want'. For him the ultimate goal of capitalism is 'to be more productive all the time', thereby constantly increasing the efficiency and wealth produced by the system. This will create some winners (the productive ones) and losers (the less productive ones), but as Buffett says, 'I'm afraid a capitalist system will always hurt some people.' It is the argument we started the chapter with: let the billionaires create the wealth first and once they have done their magic, we can use politics, taxation and charitable giving to make sure that this wealth is redistributed to those who have lost out.[22]

This argument ignores the fact that the class system, which allows one person to give so much away, is the very system that creates poverty in the first place. For example, tax avoidance costs governments across the world $500 billion each year in lost tax revenues. This is enough money to give access to clean energy for 3 billion people (£347 billion), universal access to clean water for the 2 billion that don't currently have it ($45 billion a year), tackle major infectious diseases such as HIV, TB, malaria ($89 billion a year), and still leave $19 billion in small change.[23]

Or if you think the current system is working for the majority of the world then consider this. Since 1990, global GDP has grown by 65 per cent, but the number of poor people living on less than $5 a day has actually increased, by more than 370

22   www.nytimes.com/2019/05/05/business/warren-buffett-capitalism.html, (last accessed 09/2019).

23   http://longreads.tni.org/state-of-power-2019/concentrating-wealth-and-power (last accessed 09/2019).

million. This is because the poorest 60 per cent of humanity only receive 5 per cent of this new income. At this rate, it would take 207 years to eradicate poverty at the level of $5 a day. And global GDP would need to be at 175 times the level it is at today – practically impossible given the environmental catastrophe such drastic growth and expansion would entail. For the poorest two-thirds of humanity to earn $5 a day, the average income would have to be $1.3 million per year.[24] Instead of a rising tide lifting all boats, we have a tsunami lifting yachts while the rest must suffer the flood.

Class is a relationship of power that weaves through and interconnects billions of people's lives across the world. The class forces that keep the majority of the world from having their voices heard and their pockets and bellies full are the same forces that prop up the share prices of the largest companies and the wealthiest portfolios. Warren Buffett summarised it best himself: 'There's class warfare, all right, but it's my class, the rich class, that's making war, and we're winning.'[25]

24   Jason Hickel, *The Divide: A Brief Guide to Global Inequality and its Solutions* (William Heinemann, 2017), p. 58.

25   www.nytimes.com/2006/11/26/business/yourmoney/26every.html (last accessed 09/2019).

Chapter 5

Culture: From class conundrums to class ceilings

Young people are said to be the distracted generation; growing up in a world of instantaneous gratification, where everything is on demand. For most TV executives and advertisers, this has induced nothing short of an existential crisis, as they fear millennials, unable to sit down for five minutes, will abandon live TV forever.

It is for this reason that the success of UK reality show, *Love Island*, has become something of a life saver for the TV industry, proving that the right content can still draw millions of young people in for an hour each day over eight weeks even during the hottest summer on record (as it was in 2018).[1] That year, even the Conservative Party tried to cash in on the popularity of the programme in an attempt to boost their dismal voting records among the young, making a knock off version of the sell-out *Love Island* water bottles. (The Tory knock offs, which carried slogans such as 'Don't let Corbyn Mug you off', were quickly taken down after sales flopped.)

---

1 Over half the audience of *Love Island* are in the 'hard to reach' 16 to 34 age bracket.

Like most reality TV shows, the *Love Island* audience are invited to judge the contestants as soon as they arrive on screen:[2] are they attractive, real, fake, kind, loyal? But more than this, the audience will have started to make up their minds – based on each contestant's accent, personality and presentation – about which class they belong to.

This is an understanding of class that seems at odds with the discussion so far in this book, where we have looked at class as a relationship of power that relates to work, ownership and wealth across the global economy. What do accent and personality have to do with capital and labour? This gets to the heart of a common debate around class: is class about your position in the economy or about cultural signifiers such as accents, fashion, taste, language, diet and more?

The class conundrum

In 2018 more people applied for *Love Island* than for Oxbridge, which means winning the show is no small feat. The triumphant couple that year was sparkling white-toothed Jack Fincham and straight-talking Dani Dyer – the daughter of EastEnders actor and media celebrity Danny Dyer.

Danny Dyer's public image is the stereotypical, masculine, working-class 'geezer'. Raised by a single parent in the East End of London, before becoming an actor[3] and moving to Essex, he has recently achieved fame playing the landlord of the famous Queen Vic pub in *EastEnders*. For many people, Danny Dyer is a rare and refreshing working class voice in a TV industry

---

2   The show takes a group of young single people looking for love, romance and Instagram fame, as the winning couple, as voted by viewers, wins £50,000.

3   Danny Dyer was actually mentored by Nobel Prize-winning playwright and poet Harold Pinter.

dominated by the middle class, whether he is interviewing reformed gangsters, terrorists and bouncers on the violence of their previous lives in *Danny Dyer's Deadliest Men*, or spontaneously slipping cockney rhyming slang into *EastEnders* against the wishes of its 'middle-class' writers.[4]

Danny Dyer represents a conundrum for the class analysis of this book. Which class does he belong to? Culturally speaking, he represents a very clear and reproduced working-class personality. But Danny Dyer is also a celebrity millionaire and therefore by any economic understanding of class, he is part of the middle class. So, which is it?

Before we answer this question, given that we have looked at some cultural stereotypes of the working class, it is only fair to do the same for the middle class. What does a middle-class person look like? We might have a clear idea of some middle-class traits, but even the most defining cultural characteristics of class can quickly become slippery. On the one hand a middle-class person is embodied by a character like Jeremy Clarkson – former co-presenter of TV show *Top Gear*: a middle-aged man reading the *Daily Mail*, living in the home counties, buying a sports car in a mid-life crisis, voting Conservative, gorging on red meat and rugby, etc. But we can also imagine a middle-class person that embodies the complete opposite of these things: university educated; liberal-left; enjoys eating avocados and quinoa; cares about the environment; cycles; wears Birkenstocks; drinks oat-milk flat whites; likes foreign films, etc. There are in fact many different cultural representations of both the middle and working class.

---

4 Danny Dyer clearly sees himself coming from a different class than the writers of the show who he refers to as 'quite middle class people so I'm constantly changing the dialogue and I'm freaking their nut out and they have meetings over the word "boat race" [cockney rhyming slang for "face"].'

Understanding class purely along cultural lines often leaves us unable to properly tackle and challenge where power really lies in the UK today. We are left with stereotypes that are reproduced by a media that is dominated by the upper classes (as we shall see in Chapter 8 on The Authorities, nearly half of all newspaper columnists went to private school despite only 7 per cent of the population being privately educated). These stereotypes tend to reinforce a white, male stereotype of class that almost always looks back to a nostalgic past rather than the conditions of inequality and power today. Focusing purely on the cultural connotations of class reproduces the stereotypes of decades ago, preventing us from understanding how class relations change over time, how class is neither solely white nor male and speaks with many different accents and languages.

Also, the focus on culture is so often reproduced by the media to try and undermine the potential power of working people in this country. We see this clearly with somebody like Alan Sugar, who is often presented as a working-class hero, having grown up in a poor Jewish immigrant family in Hackney before leaving school at 16 to go on to build a successful business that would turn him into a millionaire by his early 30s. His working class credentials, however, sit oddly with the fact that he is now a billionaire, member of the House of Lords, has the catchphrase 'you're fired' and goes on tirades against the poor, saying in 2015:

Who are the poor these days? You've got some people up north and in places like that who are quite poor, but they all have mobile phones, being poor, and they've got microwave ovens, being poor, and they've got televisions, being poor. Compare that to 60 years ago. If you really want to know what poor is like, go and live where I lived in Hackney, where you didn't have enough money for the electric, didn't have a shilling for the meter.[5]

Whether it's Danny Dyer or Alan Sugar, it's fair to say that the cultural signifiers of class reproduced by the media can be extremely misleading, propagating the idea that famous billionaires are working class, while say, an office worker that happens to enjoy opera might not be. With this, it is fair to conclude that Danny Dyer occupies a middle-class position in society due to his fame and wealth, despite not fitting into either of the middle-class images above.

The class ceiling

This is not to say that culture does not matter at all. 'How you come across' can be an important driver of who ends up rich and in the powerful positions in the economy. If you ever discuss class, the conversation is likely to turn to a discussion on meritocracy – the idea that those who end up in the best positions do so because they are the best. Or to phrase it more brutally, those who end up poor and in the worst jobs are the least talented. What is clear is that in order for there to be a meritocratic system, there needs to be social mobility. And if there is one thing that people agree on across the political spectrum, it is that Britain is not a very socially mobile place. It explains why in 2010 one of the first things the Conservative and Liberal Democrat coalition did was set up a Social Mobility Commission. The latest chair of the Commission, Dame Martina Milburn, articulated the aims of the commission in their latest report: 'Politicians, employers and educators all need to work together to ensure that Britain's

---

5   www.mirror.co.uk/news/uk-news/alan-sugar-says-no-poor-6564425 (last accessed 09/2019).

elite becomes more diverse in gender, ethnicity and social background. It is time to close the power gap and ensure that those at the top can relate to and represent ordinary people.'[6]

In fact, Britain was deemed so socially immobile by the commission in 2017, that the whole team actually quit in protest at the lack of government action on the issue. In their last report before quitting they wrote a candid summary of their findings, 'Whole sections of society feel they are not getting a fair chance to succeed, because they are not. It cannot go on like this.'[7]

Let us look at an example of how cultural traits can help create such a class ceiling that stops people getting into the top jobs. Go back for a moment to those TV executives we started this chapter with. Getting a commissioning job at a major TV company is one of the most illustrious jobs in the creative industry. Commissioning editors decide what millions of people will watch and therefore have the power to speak directly to people in their homes and shape the collective consciousness of the country.

In 2019, researchers from the London School of Economics, Sam Friedman and Daniel Laurison, published a book called *The Class Ceiling*, summing up years of research on exactly this relationship between cultural aspects of class and social mobility.[8] They were given unparalleled access to Channel 4 and interviewed a top senior commissioner at the broadcaster to find out how he got to the top of the company. Mark (not his real name) was honest about many of the economic privileges that helped him along the way: a private school education, a place

---

6   The Sutton Trust, *Elitist Britain 2019 The educational backgrounds of Britain's leading people* (The Sutton Trust and Social Mobility Commission, 2019).

7   Social Mobility Commission, *State of the Nation 2017: Social Mobility in Great Britain* (November 2017).

8   Sam Friedman and Daniel Laurison, *The Class Ceiling: Why it Pays to be Privileged* (Policy Press, 2019).

at a top university and the 'bank of Mum and Dad' to secure London rent while he navigated the precarious world of the creative arts. He recounts how those without this crucial safety net ended up having to take safer and more stable jobs within the industry, such as more administrative roles but with less career progression. In his own words, without such privileges the risk of going for the top job would have been like 'sky diving without a parachute'.

But what Friedman and Laurison found was that these economic privileges were not the only help Mark had. In the competitive environment of a Channel 4 commissioning room, it is not just how good you are at the job that matters. What also matters is how well you can perform a set of cultural codes. The researchers who were interviewing Mark found that he could act in a certain way that had nothing to do with how well he could do the job, but which signalled to others that he belonged in the club. As Mark recounts, 'The rules are that it's good to be right, but it's better to be funny.' Knowing when to swear or knowing in what context to put your feet on the desk could go a long way to being respected – codes that had been learned at private school.

The researchers found similar ideas across a range of industries: architecture firms, acting, and accountancy. At the top of society, culture matters for class. Even those from less privileged backgrounds who went to the same university, got the same degree and entered the same profession, ended up in a lower paid and less powerful roles in part due to these cultural codes. The authors refer to this as the class pay gap. In some cases, particularly when it intersected with race and gender, the gap was vast. For example, black British women with working-class origins who are socially mobile and find a job in the top professions still earn £20,000 a year less than white men in the same jobs but who come from a privileged background![9] It pays to be privileged.

A cup of tea

In Britain it is often said that you can tell someone's class by how they drink a cup of tea. Even Danny Dyer, as he moves from East End 'geezer' to household fame, seems to understand his changing class position by the tea he drinks, 'I don't know what's happened to me. I've got a bit more sophisticated in my old age. I like a bit of jasmine tea. I love it.'

A rigid distinction that says class is just about economics or culture is clearly a false binary. The distinction between the two is blurred – economics influences culture and cultural factors can help reproduce inequalities over time. That said, treating it as a purely cultural phenomenon makes it seem like a weird, British quirk, rather than a powerful economic force that shapes the lives of everyone on the globe. Class is about global power and the vast economic inequalities it produces, rather than about manufactured, gendered and outdated images that judge people by how they take their tea. Much more interesting questions to ask are: who makes the tea, under what conditions and who ultimately is getting rich off of it?

---

9   Ibid, p. 52.

Chapter 6

Environment: 'A handful of dust'

On 8 November 2018, California started to burn. Early in the morning, along some unmarked electricity wire in the north of the State, a fire sparked that would turn out to become the deadliest ever in its history, killing at least 90 people and tearing its way through $16.5 billion worth of damages.[1] On the same day, hundreds of miles away in the south of the State, a second fire started that would eventually destroy 1,643 buildings and result in the evacuation of more than 295,000 people. The smoke from these combined fires could be seen from as far away as New York City.

Forest fires represent everything that is terrifying about climate change. As a child, burning ourselves is often the first pain we remember, leaving something innately fearful about fire. They burn through the natural and physical world, leaving behind a blackened and uninhabitable landscape, like watching the next century play out on fast forward. All that is left is a wasteland, showing us, in the words of T S Elliot's poem, 'fear in a handful of dust'.

---

1   www.washingtonpost.com/graphics/2018/national/california-wildfires-maps/ (last accessed 09/2019).

The urgency of a fire is a far cry from the dry scientific language of global warming, which talks about heat in precise and marginal terms. Whether it's the flames of the wet Amazon or the fires of the frozen Arctic, global fires have become the canary in the gold mine. If you are ever faced with a climate change denier, just try and get them to explain the growing rise of Californian fires in recent years. As author David Wallace Wells recalls, 'Of the 10 years with the most wildfire activity on record, nine have occurred since 2000.'[2]

Of the 295,000 people that were evacuated in the 2018 fires, at least two of the names cannot be ignored. Kim Kardashian and Kanye West (KimYe), were forced to abandon their $60 million mansion in the serene gated community just outside of Los Angeles, known as the Hidden Hills. The Hills is home to several Hollywood stars and celebrities, including Kylie Jenner (the world's youngest billionaire), Miley Cyrus, Britney Spears, The Weeknd and Jennifer Lopez. As the fire finally started to die down, KimYe found themselves having to put out the flames of their own publicity crisis. Reports emerged that the couple had hired a private fire team to protect their mansion, a decision they were publicly burned for, as critics raged that they should not be able to pay for protection. In an attempt to stem the crisis, Kim Kardashian appeared on *The Ellen Show* to present a $100,000 donation to a firefighter and his wife who had lost their homes in the fire, in a declaration of their devotion to the public Californian firefighting service.

Whether Kim and Kanye were wrong for going private is not really the issue here. But it does raise the question: why couldn't they rely on the public fire service to protect their home? In answering this question, we will see that the climate crisis is

2   David Wallace-Wells, *The Uninhabitable Earth: A Story of the Future* (Penguin, 2019).

a class crisis. As the world warms and becomes ever increasingly hostile to human life, the class divides that are already so prevalent will be sharpened. This is not inevitable. But there are many features in the 2018 Californian fires that show the path we are on, an allegory for a century that will be defined by its relationship to the elements.

Burning injustice

During the fires, the Californian Fire service was stretched well beyond capacity, having to call in backup from 17 other states to tackle the engulfing flames. This was in part due to the gutting of the public service in the era of privatisation. Starting in the 1980s, the US began to promote more and more private actors into the fire industry, under the neo-liberal idea that going private would improve efficiency. By 2018, the National Wildfire Suppression Association – the main lobby group for over 250 private fire-fighting companies – claimed that 40 per cent of the money going into fighting fires in the US came from private sources.[3]

If there was one company that would be responsible for pioneering the private fire service, it would be the American Insurance Group (AIG) – the world's largest insurance company. In 2005, AIG kick-started the business model of getting rich people to pay a massive premium in exchange for a bespoke team. According to the group's press release, the 'Wildfire Defence Service' serves thousands of homes across California and has been taken up by nearly half of the Forbes 400 richest Americans.[4] That AIG was behind these developments is telling.

---

3   www.theatlantic.com/technology/archive/2018/11/kim-kardashian-kanye-west-history-private-firefighting/575887 (last accessed 09/2019).
4   www.nbcnews.com/storyline/western-wildfires/wildfire-prone-states-wealthy-pay-have-private-firefighters-protect-their-n869061 (last accessed 09/2019).

Alongside its bespoke defence service, the company was also developing a financial product that would help to ultimately set the global economy on fire.

Insurance companies may sound like boring places of little importance, but they played a major part in bringing about the 2008 financial crisis – an issue to be unpacked further in the next chapter. In the lead up to the crisis, AIG was making billions from reckless financial speculation. When things turned sour, AIG had to turn to the US government for a bailout, with taxpayers forking out $182.3 billion of public money to save the insurance giant. Many of the dodgy deals that led to the AIG's problems trace back to a division in their London office, run by a man called Joseph Cassano, or as the papers call him, 'the man who crashed the world'. Despite losing billions, he left AIG without being held to account for his actions. Instead he was rewarded with a massive financial payout: $280 million in cash and an additional $34 million in bonuses.[5]

The story of the Californian forest fires is not just the usual story of privilege paying for protection. In order to fill the void left by 40 years of privatisation, the government had to rely on its bulging prison population to put out the flames. To this day, prisoners make up a vast chunk of the Californian fire service. Over 4,000 inmates, or 40 per cent, of Californian firefighters are prisoners. For their services, they are paid a token $1 a day; receive no benefits; and if they die on the job, their families are given no compensation. Employing prisoners for barely a wage saves the US government $100 million a year.[6]

---

5   10 years after the crash, *JOE CASSANO*, https://10yearsafterthecrash.com/people/joe-cassano/ (last accessed 09/2019).
6   www.muckrock.com/news/archives/2018/aug/14/ca-firefighters-prison-labor (last accessed 09/2019).

California is infamous for its dramatically oversized and inflated prison population, having grown by 750 per cent since the mid 1970s.[7] According to academic Ruth Wilson Gilmore, the cause of this growth has nothing to do with rising crime rates, which actually fell during this time. The prison population increased because the government built new prisons, in an incarceration construction frenzy that developers proudly called 'the biggest in the history of the world'.[8] The new prisons, paid for largely out of public debt that was never intended to be repaid, provided a new meaning for a state bureaucracy under threat of privatisation. We can see the legacy of this today: California spends six times the amount to put a person behind bars than it does to put them through school.[9] There are now more women in prison in California alone than there were in the United States as a whole in 1970.[10]

From flooding to rising sea levels, fires are not the only ecological threat facing us, and the science tells us that the damaging effects of climate change will intensify over the coming years. How we respond to these crises will depend on the economic and political institutions that now govern us. What we are witnessing in California is a particularly dystopian vision of the relationship between climate change and class over the coming century: a millionaire class paying for safety from a multinational corporation that crashed the global economy but was bailed out regardless by the very taxpayers who have to rely

7 www.nytimes.com/2013/08/11/opinion/sunday/californias-continuing-prison-crisis.html (last accessed 09/2019).
8 Ruth Wilson Gilmore, *Golden Gulag: Prisons, Surplus, Crisis, and Opposition in Globalizing* (University of California Press, 2007).
9 www.gobankingrates.com/making-money/economy/states-that-spend-more-on-prisons-than-education (last accessed 09/2019).
10 Angela Davis and Cassandra Shaylor, 'Race, Gender, and the Prison Industrial Complex: California and Beyond', *Meridians* 2, no. 1, (2001): 1–25.

on crumbling state protection, while growing numbers of the poor are locked up so that they become happy to risk their lives fighting the problem for just $1 a day.

Who is responsible?

If there was one year that the Global North woke up to the scale of the environmental crisis, it would be 1988: *Time* magazine enshrined the 'Endangered Earth' as their 'person' of the year; the UN set up the IPCC (the International Panel on Climate Change); and NASA Scientist James Hansen told the US Congress that they were 99 per cent sure that warming was being caused by humans. It was the year that global warming became cool.

Yet, more than three decades on, despite thousands of scientific studies, countless programmes, protests, conferences, and annual meetings with leaders from across the globe, the achievements look bleak. As the writer David Wallace Wells argues, we have emitted more carbon since 1988 than in all the centuries and millennia before it. As he says, 'we have now engineered as much ruin knowingly as we ever managed in ignorance.'[11]

Who is responsible for these emissions? The West? Adults? The US? China? The capitalist class? In 2017, a widely cited report by the Carbon Disclosure Project (CDP) called, Carbon Majors Report, was published. The report exposed that the concentration of carbon particles in the air was the outcome of a relatively small, systemically powerful and concentrated groups of companies. The researchers found that between 1988 and 2015, 71 per cent of global emissions had been caused by just 100 companies.

---

11   David Wallace-Wells, *The Uninhabitable Earth: A Story of the Future* (Penguin, 2019).

The concentration of power in such a tiny group of organisations shows the clear class divide when it comes to who is actively creating this crisis. The future of the world rests in the hands of the tiny number of elite, privileged, predominantly male managers who run these organisations. What is worrying is that we can safely assume those who make it to the top of a major fossil fuel company care a lot about the survival of their company and much less about the survival of the ecological system. The solution to tackling ecological breakdown is therefore as much about tackling this concentration of power as about technological fixes.

You might be thinking, *but surely these companies produce the things we all need to live and survive?* It is not really fair to say that responsibility lies with those who produce the energy, when it is us – the consumers – who are really driving demand. Shifting responsibility onto consumers is a policy and ethic that we understand well when it comes to climate change. In response to ecological destruction, we have focused a lot on changing the small things: banning plastic bags and straws, recycling, eating less meat and flying less. While individual action is important, it is pointless without a wider political programme of transformative change.

But as this argument has been characterised by some as somewhat of a 'cop out' on the part of consumers, let's look at consumption. Firstly, we do not all consume equally. Imagine if you ranked all the people in the world, according to their income, from the poorest person to the richest, and you then added up the total amount of carbon that was emitted from all the things they consumed over the year – from the food they eat to the cars they drive. This is exactly what researchers at Oxfam did in a report released in the days running up to the 2015 Paris Climate negotiations – the supposedly last chance for the UN process that kick-started in 1988 to achieve something. Its key statistic is worth memorising – the highest earning 10 per cent of the global population is responsible for 50 per cent of consumption emissions.[12] If this 10 per cent reduced their consumption to the level of just the average European, then global emissions would drop by 30 per cent. When it comes to responsibility – some consumers are more accountable than others.

Climate strikes

If 1988 was the year that the world woke up to the climate crisis, then 2019 was when the coffee kicked in. On Friday 20 September, millions of people in hundreds of countries across the world walked out of schools and workplaces in the largest mass protest against climate change in history. This Global Climate Strike was the latest in the international youth movement calling for urgent and lasting action to radically decarbonise the economy. In London, where over 300,000 people marched through the streets, one of the groups to take the stage that day was a collective of indigenous, black, brown and diaspora activists from countries in the Global South called Wretched of the Earth. They started their rallying cry with the following words,

'You've all heard that "our house is on fire". But for many of us, our house has been on fire for over 500 years. And it did not set itself on fire. We did not get here by a sequence of small missteps and mistakes. We were thrust here by powerful forces that drove the unequal distribution of resources and the rigged structure of our societies. The economic system that dominates

---

12 www-cdn.oxfam.org/s3fs-public/file_attachments/mb-extreme-carbon-inequality-021215-en.pdf.

us was brought about by colonial projects whose sole purpose is the pursuit of domination and profit'.[13]

The global ecological crisis did not come from nowhere – it is the result of a long history of colonial expansion and capitalist exploitation. The inequalities that started 500 years ago live on today in the fact that the countries who are most historically responsible for emissions – the rich, industrialised countries in the Global North, which according to one estimate are responsible for emitting around 70 per cent of historical global emissions – will be the last to suffer.[14] It is poor countries that historically have contributed very little to the crisis – sub-Saharan Africa, Pacific Islands, Bangladesh, India and others in the Global South – that will be most affected. In part, this is due to a cruel twist of fate, that the poorest countries are situated in the hottest and most exposed parts of the world. But their exposure is not just the result of a natural coincidence. The legacy of colonialism and the inequalities it produced have left the rich countries with more technology, resources and wealth to adapt to the changing world. They can pay, just like KimYe and their private firefighters, for protection (albeit only up to a point).

Let us look at one example of this – access to water. As glaciers melt, lakes shrink and the water cycle becomes more volatile and unpredictable, global demand for water is expected to outstrip supply by 40 per cent as soon as 2030.[15] By 2050, over half the world's population – 5 billion people – will not have good access to fresh water, with the water crisis hitting countries

---

13 https://worldat1c.org/our-house-has-been-on-fire-for-over-500-years-97fc-668dc400 (last accessed 09/2019).

14 T. A. Boden, G. Marland, and R. J. Andres, *Global, Regional, and National Fossil-Fuel CO_2 Emissions* (Carbon Dioxide Information Analysis Center, Oak Ridge National Laboratory, 2011).

15 David Wallace-Wells, *The Uninhabitable Earth: A Story of the Future* (Penguin, 2019), p. 86.

in the Global South much harder. By 2030, India will be able to meet only half of its water needs.[16]

The words of the Wretched of the Earth collective's speech reminds us that these inequalities cannot be understood as a natural disaster. They are man-made and relate to the deep racial and class-based inequalities that started in the colonial period we saw playing out in the story of Marikana in Chapter 1. Ecological breakdown is not just a future threat; it builds on the present threats that people are already facing, which in turn are linked to the historic problems of the past. Today 2.1 billion people do not have access to safe drinking water and 4.5 billion don't have water for sanitation.[17] And in India already, 600 million face water stress and 200,000 people die each year from not having enough water.[18] In 2019 in Chennai, a major city in the south east of India, the four main water reservoirs ran completely dry, leaving its nearly 8 million residents dependent on huge shipments of bottled water.

Imagine for a moment if the hundreds of thousands of people dying due to a lack of water were in Europe. Inaction after inaction over the last 40 years has in part been the result of the fact that the people who have been on the front line of the crisis have already had their lives devalued so much by the legacy of racial injustice. The fact that it is predominantly the most marginalised, poorest, people of colour who have been most affected by this crisis goes a long way to answering why so little action has been taken. It reminds us of the calls of the miner in Chapter 1 who said, 'the life of a black person . . . is so cheap'. In the words of Swedish teenage environmental activist, Greta Thunberg, 'the suffering of the many pays for the luxury of the few.'

16   Ibid.
17   Ibid.
18   Ibid.

The sinking ship

When it comes to a problem as big and overwhelming as climate change, breaking the problem down into digestible chunks can be helpful. All of the top chief executives and board members of the 100 companies causing the majority of global emissions would be able to fit into a boat the size of the Titanic – a tiny group of people, with the power to transform the history of humanity. It's a point that has been emphasised by climate activists in a phrase commonly seen at a climate camp or demo: 'The world isn't dying. It is being killed. And the people killing it have names and addresses.'

In the blockbuster hit, *Titanic*, as the ship went down and the water started to rise, the third-class passengers were kept locked down in the hull while the first and second-class passengers had first dibs on the lifeboat. As ecological breakdown becomes impossible to ignore, we see an increasing dilemma played out in our politics as to how to tackle the issue. There is a fear that we are heading down the Californian way – the entrenching of class inequality along every line, as the rich scramble to protect their worth. If we are to avoid this, we must understand that the climate crisis arises from the same system that produces our class system. In order to break out of the lower cabins and stop the ship from sinking, the concentrated power of the rich needs to be tackled.

As C. S. Lewis, the author of *The Lion, The Witch and the Wardrobe*, once said, 'Man's power over Nature, turns out to be a power exercised by some men over other men with Nature as its instrument'. From climate change to class inequality, the destruction of the world is tied up with our destruction of each other.

Chapter 7

Housing: 'Can't pay – We'll take it away'

Unless you've been living under a rock (which given the price of rents isn't completely out of the question), you are probably aware that Britain is in the middle of one of the most extreme housing crises in its history.

Take a short walk through any city or town in the UK and you can't escape its visible signs: house prices in estate agent windows way beyond what most people can afford; increasing numbers of people sleeping rough on the street; glossy luxury apartment blocks and 'new builds' gathering dust just next door to grossly overcrowded council flats. Young people are among the hardest hit – we have even earned the nickname 'generation rent', indicating that the vast majority of us will be locked in the rental market for most of our adult lives.

What is causing this crisis?

In a typically malicious attack, many of Britain's newspapers and politicians put the blame on their usual scapegoat: immigrants. The argument goes that there is simply not enough room for everyone: this country is full up. We heard this in 2012 when the then Home Secretary, Theresa May, claimed that more than a third of all new housing demand was caused by immigration.[1] The same year, the *Daily Mail* published the headline, 'Revealed: How HALF of all social housing in England goes to people born abroad'.[2] In spite of these accusations, there is absolutely no evidence that the housing crisis is caused by immigration. In fact, the *Daily Mail* was forced to amend the above headline, when it was pointed out that only 8.6 per cent of social housing went to non-British people,[3] a figure miles off from their alleged 50 per cent.

The current housing crisis really has nothing to do with population levels. In the ten years leading up to the 2008 financial crisis, Britain's house prices grew at an astronomical pace (increasing by over 200 per cent). However, during this same period, more or less enough new houses were being supplied to match the rise in Britain's population. For every four new people added to the UK's population, three new homes were built.[4] So, if the crisis isn't caused by 'too many people', then what is going on? Rather than pointing the finger at a marginalised group, let us delve into the story of why housing has become so unaffordable. To do that we need to leave the UK, and go to the home of the global housing market – the USA.

The greatest ever trade

2007 was more than a good year for John Paulson. As a top hedge fund manager on Wall Street he was used to making a bit

---

1   www.gov.uk/government/speeches/home-secretary-speech-on-an-immigration-system-that-works-in-the-national-interest (last accessed 09/2019).

2   www.theguardian.com/housing-network/2016/jan/25/is-immigration-causing-the-uk-housing-crisis (last accessed 09/2019).

3   Ibid.

4   https://positivemoney.org/issues/house-prices.

of a killing. But in 2007 Paulson made more money than anyone had ever made in the history of finance. In one single trade he made more than $4 billion – the equivalent of $10 million every single day over the whole twelve months of the year.[5] In fact, he pocketed more money than the whole of Malawi had made that year – a country with a population of around 18 million people.

Paulson became unimaginably rich by placing a massive bet on a simple stake – that millions of American's couldn't afford the homes they had just bought. It is ironic – or perhaps just deeply cynical – that the very first thing Paulson did with his four billion was to buy a mansion in The Hamptons, the Long Island neighbourhood just outside of New York, famous for its elite residents and their opulent wealth. The mansion, called Old Trees, is a 15,000 square foot 1911 Georgian mansion, sitting in a ten-acre park on the edge of Lake Agawam, complete with a guesthouse barn, pool, and tennis court. The house cost him $40 million.

Paulson made his billions by betting against the 'mortgage backed security'. If your eyes glazed over at the term 'mortgage backed security', you are not alone. As the trader played by Ryan Gosling in the Oscar winning film, *The Big Short*, explains, '"Mortgage backed securities" – it's pretty confusing right? Does it make you feel bored? Stupid? Well it's supposed to. Wall Street loves to use confusing terms to make you think only they can do what they do. Or even better – for you to just leave them the fuck alone.'

As Ryan's character suggests, behind the jargon is actually a simple economic idea. Imagine walking down the street and seeing a beautiful house up for sale. In this imaginary world you have a well-paid job and savings stashed away, so you decide to

---

5   Gregory Zuckerman, *The Greatest Trade Ever*, (Crown Publishing Group, 2009).

buy it. You head to the bank and take out a mortgage, handing over your savings and signing on the dotted line, promising to repay the loan plus the interest. For most people, this mortgage will be paid back for what feels like a lifetime (after all, the term 'mortgage' does originate from the French for 'death-pledge').

As you start life in your new home, your mortgage is just beginning its journey. In the first leg of its trip, your mortgage is forged into a mortgage backed security (MBS). To do this, the bank bundles your mortgage together with thousands of other people's debts to create a single financial product. Whoever owns the MBS then gets the money you pay each month (plus that of thousands of other borrowers). This makes it a valuable product, particularly for rich investors that want a safe place to invest their money and earn interest.

In the second leg of the trip, the bank sells the MBS (which includes your individual mortgage) to a rich investor. The bank takes a portion of this money as a fee and uses the rest of the money to lend out another fresh round of mortgages, and so the MBS cycle continues. On the face of it, this cycle of 'lend, package and shift' seems like a win-win situation for everyone. You win by having the house of your dreams; the investor wins by receiving those nice mortgage repayments you pay each month; and the bank wins by extracting a fee every time they repackage a new MBS. This was certainly the view in Wall Street at the beginning of the twenty-first century; the MBS had turned housing into a lucrative financial asset and everyone was winning, weren't they?

John Paulson did not buy into the fairy tale. Believing that all of this seemed too good to be true, he began to investigate a bit further, and looked at who was actually taking out all of this debt. What he found was a ticking time bomb.

The banks had realised that the more mortgages they lent, packaged and sold, the more profits and bonuses they could make. To say they didn't hold back would be a gross understatement. In 2006, Wall Street was knee deep in MBS, with its bankers making $60 billion just in bonuses in that year alone. By the next Christmas this had increased to $66 billion.[6] However, in their frenzied rush to make profit, the banks had got sloppy. They had lent out astronomical sums of money to people who simply did not – and probably never would – have the income to pay their debts back.

What Paulson identified, was that within a matter of months millions of Americans would be unable to repay the loans, the MBS would lose their value, and like a house of cards, everyone who had invested in the US housing market would see their fortunes tumble. Faced with this realisation of impending collapse, he did what any self-respecting Wall Street hedge fund manager would do – he placed a bet that the whole system was about to come crashing down. And he was right.

By 2007 millions of American homeowners were unable to repay their loans. The banks and investors who had bought MBS suddenly saw their wealth vanish. Banks went bankrupt, firms stopped hiring, people stopped spending, stock prices fell, house prices plummeted and the whole system ground to a juddering halt. In the US alone, $22 trillion of wealth disappeared (for some understanding of how astronomically large this is, remember that the 2,153 billionaires in the world today currently own 'only' $8.7 trillion[7]).

The crisis spread quickly throughout the world. British, European and Asian banks had also invested heavily in MBS and

---

6   Adam Tooze, *Crashed: How a Decade of Financial Crises Changed the World*, (London: Allen Lane, 2019).

7   www.forbes.com/billionaires/#2e1e4e35251c, (last accessed 09/2019).

soon found themselves on the brink of bankruptcy. As global trade collapsed from 33 per cent to only 3 per cent of global GDP,[8] firms started to close and ordinary workers were fired. Between 2008 and 2015, 61 million people across the globe lost their jobs due to the shock. It was the worst global economic crisis since the Great Depression in the 1930s.

'Socialism for the rich and capitalism for the rest'

While removal trucks were transferring John Paulson's possessions to his new $41.3 million mansion, many of his fellow citizens were about to be made homeless. In an attempt to recover their losses, banks and investors evicted anyone unable to repay their debts, in a process known as 'foreclosure'. It wasn't just a few rogue debt collectors doing this: between 2006 and 2014, nearly 10 million homeowners in America were forced out of their homes.[9] African Americans were more than twice as likely as white borrowers to be evicted. Alongside immigrants, they have been historically excluded from the US housing market and had therefore been given the most expensive loans in the run up to the crisis.[10] The title of a Channel 5 fly-on-the-wall TV programme on the subject articulates the message sent from Wall Street to American debtors: 'Can't pay – We'll take it away.'

The banks, however, did not suffer the same fate. They were not kicked out the door and left to fend for themselves. At the point where the whole global financial system was staring into the abyss of bankruptcy, governments across the world stepped

---

8   Adam Tooze, *Crashed: How a Decade of Financial Crises Changed the World*, p. 163.
9   www.businessinsider.com/heres-where-those-who-lost-homes-during-the-us-housing-crisis-are-now-2018-8?r=US&IR=T, (last accessed 09/2019).
10   Adam Tooze, *Crashed: How a Decade of Financial Crises Changed the World*, p. 157.

in to save them with a massive taxpayer funded bailout. When we think about the bailout today, we imagine it as a one-off injection – like reviving a patient with a massive shot of adrenaline. But in reality it is much like an ongoing support system that requires constant work and attention to keep the patient alive. Right until this very day, governments continue to support the global finance system with what is known as the 'too big to fail' subsidy. The biggest banks are considered so systemically important that they know the government would have no option but to bail them out if they ever failed. Having this unofficial backing from global governments has radically affected the attitudes of the banks. Picture an extremely powerful mafia boss gambling at a local casino that relies on him for protection – his power over the casino gives him a safety net, meaning that he will take bigger risks using bigger sums of money.

According to financial news outlet Bloomberg, by no means a radical left wing source, this 'too big to fail' subsidy from taxpayers in the US alone works out at $83 billion a year – much higher than the $31.4 billion Wall Street paid itself in bonuses in 2017.[11] In other words, the banks' bonuses are only possible because of a government hand out. It's what economist Robert Reich calls, 'Socialism for the rich and capitalism for the rest'.[12]

What is a house?

The crisis and its aftermath raise a question that we need to answer if we are to understand Britain's housing crisis: what is the point of a house? You might think the answer is blindingly obvious: houses are for shelter, a place to come to after school

11 https://www.bloomberg.com/opinion/articles/2013-02-20/why-should-tax payers-give-big-banks-83-billion-a-year- (last accessed 09/2019).
12 Ibid.

and do homework, to rest, sleep, cook and watch Netflix. A house is surely a home. But houses are not just homes. If they were, how could we possibly explain why millions of families were evicted from their homes following the financial crisis and taken over by a bank? Banks are, after all, not people: they don't need beds or gardens. From the lender handing out mortgages, to investors buying up MBS, houses have become a financial asset – something to be bought and sold. Not just a place to live, but a commodity that generates profit. These two meanings of what a house is do not always sit well together. In fact, the more that houses are viewed as a commodity, the less they can function as a home.

Focus E15

The commodification of homes was challenged by a group of young working-class mothers in the London Borough of Newham in 2014. It had been over half a decade on from the financial crisis, and the government, which had pumped billions into the banking system, were now slashing public budgets – an issue discussed in further detail in the next chapter. A tiny sliver of these cuts fell on a hostel providing rundown temporary accommodation for homeless young women and children in the borough, called Focus E15. As the government withdrew £41,000 in funding for the hostel, the women and their children were told to pack up their belongings and leave. Where exactly they would go was not clear. Newham council would not give them social housing in London and threatened to relocate them to other British towns and cities, hundreds of miles from their family, jobs and support networks.

The Focus E15 mums decided to take matters into their own hands. Nearby, on the edge of the new glittering Olympic Village, sat a block of old council houses, which had lain empty for years. Newham Council had kicked out the previous occupants with plans to demolish the homes and sell the land on to private developers. Even though the flats were simply sitting there, the council were happy to do nothing, watch the price increase and wait for the highest bidder. In many areas of London, simply buying property and leaving it vacant will generate enough returns to make a profit. One estimate suggests that half of 'new builds' in London are left empty[13] – a damning indictment in a city where more than 6,000 people sleep rough on the streets each night.[14]

In the autumn of 2014, the mums took their prams in one hand and their protest signs in the other and occupied the estate. By reclaiming the empty flats, they transformed them overnight from a speculative asset back into homes. To their surprise the mums found that many of the 600 empty flats on the estate were in good shape, certainly better than the damp, prison like rooms of the Focus E15 hostel. They hung banners, organised workshops and refused to leave until they were adequately housed. It was de-commodification in action. As one banner read, 'These people need homes, these homes need people'.

While occupying empty buildings will not solve the housing crisis altogether (although it could certainly help to significantly reduce homelessness), the protest highlighted the many ways that housing has been commodified in the UK. Only 8 per cent of people in the UK today live in council-owned accommodation. In 'landlord Britain', the council house has been given a

---

13 Rowland Atkinson, 'Necrotecture: Lifeless Dwellings and London's Super Rich', *The International Journal of Urban and Regional Research* 43, no. 1, (January 2019): 2–13.
14 S. Fitzpatrick, H. Pawson, G. Bramley, S. Wilcox, B. Watts and J. Wood, *The Homelessness Monitor: England 2018* (London: Crisis, 2018).

bad reputation, represented as a den of poverty and anti-social behaviour, as the derogatory slur 'CHAV' indicates – thought by some to be a slur for 'council housed and violent'.

Yet the association of council houses with crime and poverty is only a recent phenomenon. Back in 1979, a staggering 42 per cent of the population lived in council housing.[15] During this period, council homes were owned by the government, could not be bought and sold, and were used for one purpose: to provide a place for people to live at rents they could afford. But this changed dramatically in 1980 when then Prime Minister Margaret Thatcher introduced a law that would prove to be revolutionary. The 'right to buy' policy allowed (and in fact encouraged) anyone living in council accommodation to buy their property, transforming millions of homes into commodities – things to be bought and sold on a market. Over the course of 25 years, 1.5 million council homes were sold off via 'right to buy', making it the UK's biggest ever privatisation of state assets.[16] Just like the MBS system, the first few years were presented as a win-win for all: millions of working people could, for the first time, own their own place and join the ranks of the so called 'aspiring middle class'. The government got a big payout and the sniff of a housing boom got everyone dizzy at the thought of becoming a wealthy homeowner.

Yet the celebrations did not last long. The UK government never rebuilt the council houses it sold off, leading to a chronic undersupply of affordable housing. Over the next few decades, the housing market expanded and the price of homes kept going up and up. This process was helped out by the loosening of mortgage lending and the rise of MBS, just like in the US.

---

15   www.theguardian.com/society/2016/jan/04/end-of-council-housing-bill-secure-tenancies-pay-to-stay (last accessed 09/2019).

16   www.lrb.co.uk/v36/n01/james-meek/where-will-we-live (last accessed 09/2019).

Remember that at the beginning of this chapter, we said that UK house prices rose by 200 per cent in the ten years leading up to the financial crisis. We asked the question, if this wasn't caused by immigration, then what was it caused by? Now we can answer the question. It has been driven almost exclusively by an increase in mortgage lending by UK banks. With more lending, people can always pay a higher price – a bit like using a phone contract to buy the new £1000+ iPhone, even without any savings or a great job. Billions of new mortgages were issued and bundled together into MBS and sold to rich investors across the world. From 1999 to 2007, the value of MBS issued in the UK rose from 2 per cent of GDP to 27 per cent of GDP.[17]

By the late 90s, a new term had been coined: 'buy to let'. These new 'buy to let' landlords were purchasing more and more houses they never intend to live in or call home – a symbol of the triumph of the commodification of housing. Since 1999, the number of 'buy to let' landlords has increased by over 2,500 per cent.[18] This in turn has dramatically increased the price of rents: in the 1960s and 70s, renters would spend on average around one tenth of their income on housing; by 2016 this had risen to over a third.[19]

'Generation Rent'

The Focus E15 mums were not simply fighting for their own right to a council house. They were exposing how fundamentally

---

17 Josh Ryan–Collins, *Why Can't You Afford a Home?* (The Future of Capitalism) (Polity Press, 2018).

18 www.theguardian.com/money/2015/jan/12/the-housing-crisis-in-charts (last accessed 09/2019).

19 David Willetts et al, *A New Generational Contract: The final report of the Intergenerational Commission* (Resolution Foundation, 2018).

broken the housing system has become. In particular their experience as young working class single mothers resonated across their peer group. 'Generation rent' is now an established term, with the government releasing the first government inquiry into the issue in 2019. According to the inquiry, if things carry on as they are, our generation will on average remain trapped in the extortionate private rental market throughout our lifetime. In retirement, we will be forking out on average 80 per cent of our income in rent.[20] As activist and author George Monbiot says, 'People say "I work for Tesco" or "I work for Deliveroo", but the reality for many is that they work for their landlord.'[21]

Working class migrants were at the sharpest end of this banker-generated mess, and yet they are the first to be blamed for a crisis they did not create. They have been scapegoated in order to hide the real problem at the heart of the housing crisis: the commodification of housing. By turning houses into property, they have failed to fulfil their functions as homes: whether it's in the aftermath of the financial crisis in the US, evicting families to protect the profits of banks, or the selling off of council homes in the UK. In short, housing has become just another way for the richest in society to get even richer.

20   Richard Best and Anya Martin, *Rental Housing For An Ageing Population*, APPG Housing and Care for Older People, government report (July 2019).
21   www.theguardian.com/commentisfree/2019/jul/17/housing-britain-landlord-tenants, (last accessed 09/2019).

Chapter 8

The authorities: Schools, prisons and the welfare state

On a sunny day in June 2018, over 900 students and staff from St Paul's Girls' School – one of Britain's leading private schools – headed into their dining room and sat down for lunch. Usually the food at St Paul's reads like the menu at a Michelin Star restaurant: slow-baked Moroccan lamb, duck leg confit and seared cod.[1] That day, however, the students were greeted by something a little more tasteless. The school was serving what it called an 'austerity lunch': jacket potatoes, beans and coleslaw. The reason for this 'basic' food was, in the words of the school, to 'raise the awareness of our students to those less fortunate than themselves'.

After the government spent billions bailing out the banks following the 2008 financial crisis, the New Coalition government in 2010 implemented a programme of extensive budget cuts that later came to be known as austerity. For the last ten years, these cuts have been the defining economic policy of the

---

1 www.dailymail.co.uk/news/article-5874703/St-Pauls-Girls-School-slammed-serving-pupils-baked-potatoes-beans-AUSTERITY-DAY-lunch.html (last accessed 09/2019).

government. Nothing has come to symbolise austerity Britain more than the rise of food poverty. Between 2008 and 2018, The Trussell Trust – the UK's largest food bank – has gone from handing out just under 26,000 parcels of food each year to over 1.3 million.[2] Study after study shows that austerity is driving people into hunger.[3] Despite the government deflecting and denying any responsibility, they now even admit that there is a link, albeit they are still trying to underplay their role in the hunger crisis. In the words of food writer and campaigner Jack Monroe, 'An austerity lunch is really no lunch at all.'

St Paul's charges pupils £7,978 per term; it is a finishing school for those who are most likely to end up running the country. While only 7 per cent of students in the UK go to private school, 65 per cent of senior judges, 57 per cent of the House of Lords, 53 per cent of Diplomats, 44 per cent of newspaper columnists, and 29 per cent of MPs are all privately educated.[4] From the schools, to the criminal justice system to the state – these are the people who will be in charge. They are the authorities.

In the class(ed)room

The journey from Britain's private schools into the ranks of high office is well trodden and will likely pass through either Oxford or Cambridge. Take St Paul's as an example. It is one of eight schools that send more pupils to Oxbridge than *three quarters* of

---

2   www.hrw.org/report/2019/05/20/nothing-left-cupboards/austerity-welfare-cuts-and-right-food-uk, (last accessed 09/2019).

3   Rachel Loopstra and Doireann Lalor, *Financial insecurity, food insecurity, and disability: The profile of people receiving emergency food assistance from The Trussell Trust Foodbank Network in Britain*, University of Oxford's Economic and Social Research Council Report (2017).

4   The Sutton Trust, *Elitist Britain 2019 The educational backgrounds of Britain's leading people*, Report, The Sutton Trust and Social Mobility Commission (2019).

the rest of schools in the whole country. While less than 1 per cent of the adult population goes to Oxbridge, over 24 per cent of the top jobs in the country are taken up by Oxford graduates.[5]

Private schools are as much about class segregation as they are about actually providing a better education. The segregation is obvious and blunt: a barrier is erected that most people cannot jump over – i.e. annual fees that are higher than the disposable income of the average English family[6] – creating a small and selected pool of wealthy elites that have first dibs on the top jobs, like buying a first class plane ticket.

This is not to say that parents send children to private school only because they want their children to mix with the wealthy. Undoubtedly private schools do provide much better resources, smaller class sizes and the rest, which in turn are linked to a better education. But there is little evidence that if private schools were integrated into the state system and the rich ended up having to go to state schools – a policy which the Labour Party adopted at its 2019 conference – that the education they received would be drastically worse. Finland successfully abolished private schools and integrated them into the state system over a course of a decade starting in the early 1970s. The attainment gap between the richest and poorest students closed, not because the wealthy students became worse, but because the poorer students did better. This is one of the reasons why Finland is widely cited as having one of the best education systems in the world.[7]

That said, even if we did nationalise Eton, would the class divisions in the education system simply disappear? Given the

5   Ibid.
6   www.theguardian.com/news/2018/aug/24/the-only-way-to-end-the-class-divide-the-case-for-abolishing-private-schools, (last accessed 09/2019).
7   Pasi Sahlberg, *Finnish Lessons: What Can the World Learn from Educational Change in Finland? (The Series on School Reform)* (Teachers' College Press, 2012).

level of class segregation in our state school system, the answer is likely, no. Take grammar schools for example, which do not charge fees and are funded by the state, but select students based on their ability to pass an exam at the age of eleven. Grammar schools have been largely phased out of the British education system. In the mid 1960s, over a quarter of state school students attended grammar school, while today it is less than five per cent.[8] Those that remain defend their existence on the idea that they are truly meritocratic – providing a better education to those who are more naturally talented and gifted.

The issue with grammar schools is very similar to that with private schools: what might seem like a meritocratic education system looks more like a way to segregate people by classes. Six per cent of grammar school pupils qualify for free school meals, compared to the average of 14.6 per cent.[9] The reason for this is simple: with enough private tutoring you can effectively buy your way into passing the eleven plus exams or, if you are wealthy enough, afford to move into the catchment areas of these schools where the house prices tend to be high. Moreover, research by Durham University shows that going to a grammar school does not actually give you a better education. Once students' class backgrounds and their attainment levels at age eleven are taken into account, those that go to grammar school do not seem to do any better than those that do not.

So, what if we abolished grammar schools *and* private schools? It would certainly help to tackle class inequality in our education system. However, even within the supposedly egalitarian state-funded comprehensive school system, our classrooms are still

---

8   Paul Bolton, *Grammar School Statistics* (House of Commons Library, Briefing Paper, no. 1398, 2017).
9   Stig Abel, *How Britain Really Works: Understanding the Ideas and Institutions of a Nation* (John Murray, 2019).

split along class lines. Take the issue of streaming people into different sets. Again, this is justified along the lines that separating people according to their intelligence helps to improve the quality of everyone's education. But again, the same problem arises. The top sets, considered smarter and higher up the social hierarchy, are populated disproportionately by richer students. For example, 46 per cent of middle class students with high IQs are put in the top set at school, compared to only ten per cent of similarly smart kids from working class backgrounds.[10] Everything from how children are judged by teachers, to the type of content children are actually interested in learning about, are all impacted by class. In short, class can get you a long way in the classroom.

Ultimately, running through all these issues is a common problem: an attempt to split people according to some standard (ability) becomes a way to split people according to class. The veneer of meritocracy masks the class-based inequalities at the heart of our school system, implying that those who make it to the top (whether it be a top set, grammar school or private school) are inherently better than the rest. In doing so it ignores the structural inequalities at the heart of our system that have only been compounded by austerity. In its own research the Department for Education found that cuts to school budgets were hitting the poorest students the hardest. For example, secondary schools where more than 40 per cent of children are on free school meals have had average cuts per pupil of £803 – that is £326 more cuts than the average secondary school in the country.[11]

---

10 Diane Raey, *Miseducation: Inequality, education and the working classes*, Policy Press, 2017
11 Ibid.

The penal system: 'We are a protected species'

School failed me, and I failed the school. It bored me. The teachers behaved like [officers]. I wanted to learn what I wanted to know, but they wanted me to learn for the exam. What I hated most was the competitive system there, and especially sports. Because of this, I wasn't worth anything, and several times they suggested I leave.

This kind of disillusionment is rife in our rigid and disciplinary school system. While this quote could easily have come from one of the 35 pupils who are expelled each day in the UK, it's actually from someone else: Albert Einstein. Einstein was kicked out of school at the age of 15 after a heated argument with his teacher, but still went on to win a Nobel Prize in Physics, achieving such intellectual heights that his surname has become a synonym for genius. If he was educated in Britain today, he might well have ended up behind bars.

Being excluded from school is one of the biggest determinants of ending up in prison: more than half of UK prisoners have previously been expelled.[12] As Martin Narey, the former director of HM Prison services said, 'The 13,000 young people excluded from school each year might as well be given a date by which to join the prison service sometime later down the line.'[13] It is the most disadvantaged children that end up being expelled from school: a 2019 review by the Department of Education showed that 78 per cent of expelled pupils had either special educational

---

12   Kiran Gill, with Harry Quilter-Pinner and Danny Swift, *Making the difference: Breaking the link between school expulsions and social exclusion* (The Institute for Public Policy Research, 2017).

13   Akala, *Natives: Race and Class in the Ruins of Empire* (Two Roads, 2019).

needs (SEN), were eligible for free school meals (FSM) or were 'in need'.[14]

All classes commit crimes, but the poorer you are the more likely you are to go to prison. Think for a moment of the countless crimes that have been committed by businesses and capitalists just over the last few years. Not just moral crimes that might be hard to prosecute in a court of law, such as the ongoing destruction of the planet or the arms sales to authoritarian leaders. But actual criminal activity that is easier to pin down in our current legal system.

In 2012, a US federal investigation found HSBC responsible for laundering at least $881 million for the Mexican Sinaloa drug cartel (run by the billionaire El Chapo we met in back in Chapter 4).[15] Despite the investigators discovering that 'that senior bank officials were complicit in the illegal activity',[16] the US attorney general decided not to prosecute the bank. This came after a huge diplomatic campaign waged by the UK government, whose Chancellor of Exchequer at the time, George Osborne, cried wolf that touching the bank might risk 'global financial disaster'.[17] HSBC was let off with a tiny fine and a slap on the wrist, corroborating the words of a top financial executive at the time, 'I can assure you if you think Her Majesty's Government is ever going to prosecute people of my class, you are utterly mistaken. We are a protected species.'[18]

---

14   Edward Timpson, *Timpson Review of School Expulsion*, government review (2019).

15   www.ft.com/content/58775414-de5a-11e7-a8a4-0a1e63a52f9c, (last accessed 09/2019).

16   www.theguardian.com/commentisfree/2012/dec/12/hsbc-prosecution-fine-money-laundering (last accessed 09/2019).

17   https://financialservices.house.gov/uploadedfiles/07072016_oi_tbtj_sr.pdf.

18   Nicholas Shaxson, *The Finance Curse: How global finance is making us all poorer* (Random House, 2018).

If so many in the upper classes are able to dodge a prison sentence, who are the 82,400 locked away in prison in England and Wales today?[19] While HBSC executives might not be doing their time for laundering drug money, many predominantly working class and communities of colour are paying a heavy toll for the war on drugs. Inspector Nick Glynn, vice president of the National Black Police Association, summarises how class, race and the justice system really works, 'If you aren't well off – if you're young, from an urban area, black, or Asian – your chances of getting stopped by the police for drugs are much higher.'

Most stop and searches (two thirds) are reportedly about drugs, and are mainly targeted at the poor and unemployed. In London, incidents of stop and search are concentrated in deprived areas of the city, with 93 per cent of those who were stopped and searched in 2013 coming from 'lower socio-economic groups'. Compounding this unfairness is the fact that if you are, for example, a banker, doctor or lawyer and happen to be caught with drugs, you are more much less likely to be stop and searched in the first place. And on the rare chance that this group is stopped, they are three times more likely to be let off with a caution than those who are unemployed[20] – a protected species indeed.

The intersection between class and race is critical when it comes to the justice system. In London, black people are stopped and searched at nine times the rate of white people, despite the fact that they represent a much smaller part of the population, use drugs at a lower rate and are less likely to actually be found

---

19   England and Wales have the highest prison rates in Western Europe – more than three times the amount in Italy and Spain. Prison Reform Trust, *Prison: the facts Bromley Briefings Summer 2019*, report (2019).

20   www.vice.com/en_us/article/a38a45/britains-upper-classes-are-less-likely-to-be-busted-for-drugs (last accessed 09/2019).

with anything on them. As a black person, if you are found in possession of something, you are more likely to be arrested, eight times more likely to be prosecuted and nine times more likely to be sent to prison. This is why over 40 per cent of young people in custody are from BAME (Black and minority ethnic) backgrounds, despite only making up 14 per cent of the population.[21]

The criminal justice system reproduces the racial and class inequalities that exist in our society. Sometimes it's easier to think of this as a 'broken' system – an institutional failure to deal with the complexities of crime in our challenging world. Yet, the more one thinks about it, the more it feels like things are not broken. They are working actually as they are supposed to. Think about it. The prison system fails at protecting communities from crime. It fails terribly at rehabilitating people. It's obscenely expensive – as the rapper and social critic, Akala, has pointed out, 'It costs more to send a child to prison then it does to send them to Eton'.[22]

So why does our failing and expensive system continue? In short, because it does a good job at punishing those at the bottom who step out of line. We see this clearly in the words of those who run the country, whether it is Home Secretary Priti Patel who says she wants 'criminals to feel terror' or Home Office Minister Victoria Atkins who claims that social housing should be taken away from the parents of criminals so that they 'understand the consequences of their criminal behaviour'. These threats have an inbuilt class bias – it is fair to say that they are not talking about HSBC executives.

---

21   David Lammy, *The Lammy Review: An independent review into the treatment of, and outcomes for, Black, Asian and Minority Ethnic individuals in the Criminal Justice System*, government review (2017).

22   Grace Rahman, *Prison or Eton: which costs more?* (Full Fact: The UK's Independent Factchecking Charity, 2018).

Einstein received his Nobel Prize for discovering something known as the photoelectric effect: when a light is shone on a material, electrons are freed and escape into the air. The words of prison abolitionist and academic, Angela Davis, spring to mind: 'Prisons do not disappear social problems, they disappear human beings.'[23] How many people, including the next Einstein, are sitting in a dark cell waiting to be released?

Disability and the welfare state

Are all aspects of the state so punitive? The NHS, pensions, social housing, disability allowance, unemployment benefits, public transport, free education – are these not all examples that the authorities actually provide a decent life for those who find themselves on the poorer side of the class split?

In 1945 the country was broke and drowning in debt. This did not stop the newly elected Labour government, who had just beaten Winston Churchill at the ballot box, from implementing a series of reforms that would change the future of the country, a cradle-to-grave support system called, the welfare state. The basic principle of the welfare state was that everyone should have the things they needed to survive and flourish, regardless of which class they belonged to (although as we shall see in the next chapter, not everyone was included).

Over the last 40 years of neo-liberalism, this principle of universal access to basic goods and services has been slowly chiselled away at. Since the start of austerity in 2010, the chisel has been replaced with a wrecking ball. To understand the damage done to the welfare state, we need to look at a vital issue: disability.

---

23 Angela Davies, *Masked racism: reflections on the prison industrial complex*, *Indigenous Law Bulletin* 4, no. 27, (Feb 2000): 4–7.

Disability and poverty so often come together: over a third of all adults in poverty are disabled. Yet, unlike poverty, which under the neo-liberal narrative is blamed on the individual deficiencies of the poor – a lack of intelligence, effort, and so on – disability has generally been seen as something that happens beyond their individual control. For this reason it has been harder for the authorities to use the typical idea of 'individual responsibility' to justify taking away the benefits of disabled people. As Frances Ryan, the author of *Crippled: Austerity and the Demonization of Disabled People*, explains, 'While, say, the figure of working class jobseeker or single mother was said to "deserve" contempt, disabled people – culturally seen as pitiable and passive – were widely viewed as the "good" recipients of state help'.[24]

In austerity Britain, this is no longer the case. The authorities have waged nothing short of an all-out war on disabled people, albeit with a different strategy. Rather than arguing that disability was the result of individual personal failings, the architects of austerity have opted for the myth that those who claim disability benefits are not really disabled at all. They are, in the words of ex-Prime Minister David Cameron, 'welfare scrounger[s]'.[25] This toxic narrative has attempted to justify the unfair distribution of cuts: if you are disabled, you will face nine times more cuts than the average citizen. If you are severely disabled, this rises to 19 times.[26]

---

24   Frances Ryan, *Crippled: Austerity and the Demonization of Disabled People* (Verso, 2019).

25   www.mirror.co.uk/news/politics/dwp-extends-maximus-fit-work-14089513 (last accessed 09/2019).

26   www.centreforwelfarereform.org/uploads/attachment/354/a-fair-society.pdf (last accessed 09/2019).

Let us look at the story behind just one of these cuts. In 2013, the government abolished a benefit called the Disability Living Allowance, which was set up in 1992 to help cover extra care and mobility costs, replacing it with the Personal Independence Payment (PIP). They claimed that the old system had become 'riddled with abuse and fraud',[27] and so decided to drag three million people through a series of physical tests to root out the so-called 'liars'.

The tests turned out to be nothing more than a sham. Before they were even run, the government had already decided how many people they wanted to kick off the benefits: 500,000 or one fifth of all people receiving it.[28] This was despite the fact that all evidence at the time pointed to only a tiny fraction of cases being fraudulent, around 0.5 per cent. In other words, the government were claiming that the levels of fraud were 40 times higher than they actually were.

Out of the hundreds of thousands of people who have had their benefits cancelled, as many as 72 per cent of these cancellations have been deemed unlawful and overturned by the Court of Appeal.[29] To make matters worse, these tests have become a lucrative profit making enterprise for the two private companies that run them – Capita and Atos.[30] In just the first three years of the new tests being implemented, the government forked out £500 million to these two companies. In a normal job, if you get a decision wrong three quarters of the time, you will most likely be fired. Yet, in 2019 the government renewed the contracts

27   www.telegraph.co.uk/news/politics/9263502/Iain-Duncan-Smith-Im-not-scared-to-light-the-fuse-on-disability-reform.html (last accessed 09/2019).

28   Frances Ryan, *Crippled: Austerity and the Demonization of Disabled People.*

29   Dan Bloom, *DWP extends Maximus fit-for-work tests contract as huge benefits change revealed* (2019).

30   www.theguardian.com/commentisfree/2016/dec/27/taxpayers-cash-should-go-to-needy-ends-up-atos-capita, (last accessed 09/2019).

for Capita and Atos, guaranteeing them a stream of taxpayers' money to run bogus tests until 2021. In the meantime, hundreds of thousands of disabled people are left without the money they need to survive. Six in ten of families that have someone with a disability currently go without a basic necessity – food, shelter or heating. Five million disabled people are in poverty.[31]

'Poverty is a political choice'

Over the last decade, the authorities have told us that austerity was an economic necessity; that unless we cut the deficit, the economy would collapse and we would all be much worse off. The decision might be 'tough', but it was 'unavoidable' – like taking 'a bitter medicine'.

These have all turned out to be lies. Halfway through the programme, the government did the opposite of deficit reduction, cutting taxes and therefore its source of revenue. By the early 2020s, the government will save less from its cuts to the welfare budget (£35 billion a year) than it will lose from the tax cuts it has implemented (£47 billion per year).[32] Since it undertook austerity, the government has missed every deficit reduction target it set itself. And as for improving the economy? According to research from the Resolution Foundation, wages by 2022 still won't have reached what they were back in 2007.[33]

Austerity was never about balancing the budget. It was a class battle waged by the rich through the very nature of government

31 Frances Ryan, *Crippled: Austerity and the Demonization of Disabled People*.

32 Ibid.

33 Stephen Clarke, Adam Corlett, David Finch, Laura Gardiner, Kathleen Henehan, Daniel Tomlinson and Matt Whittaker, *Are we nearly there yet? Spring Budget 2017 and the 15 year squeeze on family and public finances*, Resolution Foundation briefing (2017).

and in whose interests its institutions are run. Austerity shifted the responsibility for the financial crisis away from the banks and speculators and onto the welfare state and the millions of people that use it. It hit the poorest hardest, while lining the pockets of the rich through tax cuts.[34] It opened up profitable business opportunities for companies like Capita, which were to administer the new punitive system. Little wonder then that during the first five years of the programme, the richest 1,000 families in the country saw their wealth double to £547 billion – more wealth than the poorest 40 per cent of British households.[35]

Things have deteriorated so much that the United Nations has visited the country to assess the damage to human rights, not once or twice, but three times (in 2016, 2017 and 2018). The findings of the latest report lays bare the logic behind what it calls these 'ideological' cuts.[36]

[P]overty is a political choice. Austerity could easily have spared the poor, if the political will had existed to do so. Resources were available to the Treasury at the last budget that could have transformed the situation of millions of

---

34 In 2013, Osborne reduced income tax for the highest income earners from 50 pence to 45 pence. This was a blessing for the country's millionaires, who according to one paper, saved on average £554,000 each from 2013 to 2018 and cost the country £8.6bn over those years. In 2010, Corporation tax was at 28 per cent – around the OECD average and much less than the US which had a corporate tax rate of nearly 40 per cent. But another of George Osborne's leaving presents was to have this reduced to 17 per cent by 2020, costing the government billions in lost revenues. www.ifs.org.uk/publications/9207 (last accessed 09/2019).

35 www.theguardian.com/business/2015/apr/26/recession-rich-britains-wealthiest-double-net-worth-since-crisis (last accessed 09/2019).

36 www.ohchr.org/documents/issues/poverty/eom_gb_16nov2018.pdf (last accessed 09/2019).

people living in poverty, but the political choice was made to fund tax cuts for the wealthy instead.[37]

This is from a formally neutral international observer. What clearer picture could there be that the government acts in the interests of the richest in our society?

---

37 Ibid.

Chapter 9

Race: 'I never thought of class applying to black people'

The common man has been abandoned, left behind and betrayed by the liberal metropolitan elite that care more about political correctness and foreigners then they do about dealing with the real problems of ordinary people.

From Trump to Brexit, this political argument has become a defining feature of mainstream politics. Right-wing movements across Europe and the US have wielded it, claiming to represent the voice of the 'real' and 'authentic' working class. Yet scratch the surface of what 'authentic' really means and the argument quickly slides into a narrative about race. Take, for example, Brexiteer Nigel Farage, who has gone from the trading floors of The City of London, to anti-establishment man of the people. In the lead up to the Brexit referendum in 2016, Farage rephrased the narrative above in blunter terms: 'Immigration has left our white working class as an underclass'.

To understand the power of this narrative, we must remember that the far right are not the only group in society that see the working class as white. In a 2018 research project young people from across the capital were interviewed about their views on race and class. Many of those interviewed were young black women – not what you might call Nigel Farage's key demographic support base – yet they too shared the idea that the working class was for white people. Joy, who is in her 20s, said, 'I never thought of class applying to black people [...] I feel like the word "white" has been attached to working class so much that, nah, I can't identify with it.' Similarly, 19-year-old Grace said, 'When I was young, I didn't think class was a real thing, I thought it was on TV, in the Victorian times, and then in sociology we were talking about class, and working-class people, you think of coalminer, white people.'[1] To understand why the language of class is so racialised we need to delve into our history, looking at four key historical moments in our past that can help us to untangle the complicated relationship between race and class.[2]

'When the first Africans arrived in Virginia in 1619, there were no "white" people there'

Britain's first colony in the Western Hemisphere was established in Virginia in 1607.[3] The ships landed on the shores carrying a small group of wealthy investors and large numbers of poor Europeans who were brought there as indentured servants (people who were contracted to work five to seven years to pay off their debts). The first Africans came to the colony in 1619, the year Virginia also established its first government and first

1 www.runnymedetrust.org/uploads/publications/We%20Are%20Ghosts.pdf (last accessed 09/2019).

2 The history of race and class in Britain and the world is much more complicated than a short chapter can do justice. For more reading, I would suggest looking into: Peter Fryer, *Staying Power: The History of Black People in Britain* (Pluto Press, 2018) and Robbie Shilliam, *Race and the Undeserving Poor* (Agenda Publishing, 2018).

3 W. Billings, 'The Law of Servants and Slaves in Seventeenth-Century Virginia', *The Virginia Magazine of History and Biography* 99, no. 1, (1991): 45–62.

tobacco farm. In these early days, of what would later become the USA, slavery did not exist. Just like their European counterparts, Africans came as indentured servants that could work their way to freedom. People were not segregated on racial lines and inter-racial relationships and marriages were commonplace. This is not to say these early years were a utopia without any discrimination. All servants were 'beaten, maimed, and even killed with impunity', in the words of black historian Barbara Fields,[4] leading many to flee and settle with the neighbouring indigenous Algonquian people.

For the British colonial elite, this was a problem. They wanted their servants to be working hard in the tobacco fields, not 'fleeing or fornicating' as they called it. The issue hit crisis point when a rebellious multi-ethnic group of servants rose up in 1676 demanding an end to indentured labour. They burned down the capital city Jamestown and forced the governor to flee back to England. After returning with an army, the rebellion was quickly crushed, and the old guard were reinstated. The uprising however had exposed the weak foundations of colonial power. The elites came to the conclusion that brute force alone would not be enough to maintain power. They needed to establish a more effective method of divide and rule.

In response to the uprising, the British implemented a new law in 1682 that for the first time defined Africans as slaves – property to be bought and sold.[5] Obviously this was not the first time humans had enslaved other humans. The Ancient Greeks, Romans, Egyptians and Moghuls all had their own systems of slavery. Unlike these lost empires though, whose impact on today's world is like a distant ripple, the ideas that legitimised

---

4   S. Virdee, 'Racialized capitalism: An account of its contested origins and consolidation', *The Sociological Review* 67, no. 1, (2019): 3–27.
5   Ibid.

the trans-Atlantic slave trade still have the capacity to send a tidal wave through our politics.

In an attempt to justify turning people into property, any relationships that existed between the European and African labourers had to be destroyed. Marriage across the two groups was outlawed. English women giving birth to the child of an African father were publicly whipped. Children born by African women would not inherit their father's status and name, a law that effectively legitimated sexual violence on a mass scale.

While these policies created some divisions, it was only a final law that ultimately separated the two groups – the invention of whiteness. By 1691 the term 'white' was first introduced into the law[6] and in the tobacco fields of Virginia, the idea of a superior white race was first used to control the population. Being 'white' gave you economic benefits regardless of which class you belonged to: whites could own land, move without a pass and marry without upper class consent.[7] Whereas being black stripped you of any rights and humanity, denigrating you as simply property to be owned. This is why historian Theodore Allen said, 'When the first Africans arrived in Virginia in 1619, there were no 'white' people there'.[8] What made the focus on race unique as a strategy for dividing people was that it pretended that the law and ownership – a human invention – was derived from some kind of natural, biological truth.

Over the course of the next few centuries, laws based on whiteness were used by the British throughout its colonies across the world. One of the first popular books justifying this new idea of race was *The History of Jamaica*, written in 1774 by

6   Asad Haider, *Mistaken Identity, Race and Class in the Age of Trump* (Verso, 2018), p. 52.
7   S. Virdee, *Racialized capitalism*.
8   Ibid.

slave owner Edward Long.[9] The book argued that Africa and the people that lived there were inherently inferior, or in Long's words, 'everything that is monstrous in nature'. These kinds of racialised ideas became so entrenched, that in the Victorian times a whole academic discipline was dedicated to theories attempting to prove the biological superiority of white people and the inferiority of non-white people.[10]

'You can't have capitalism without racism'

By the mid seventeenth century, Britain had become the dominant slave trading nation and its ability to industrialise before any other country in the world was made possible off the backs of those it enslaved.[11] The following cultural signifier of class – discussed back in Chapter 5 – can tell us much about the importance of the slave trade to Britain's economy: the humble cup of tea. Before the mid eighteenth century, tea was exclusively a luxury product for the upper classes, and just like today, they knew a cup of tea goes best with a spoonful of sugar. With the expansion of British colonialism across the globe, cups of tea became more readily available for consumers at home, with the leaves coming from Asia, and the sugar from the slave-run plantations in the Caribbean. As the human cost of a cup of tea

9 www.theguardian.com/commentisfree/2015/sep/08/european-racism-africa-slavery (last accessed 09/2019).

10 Even Europe was split into races – Nordic, Roman, Gallic, Slavic and Semitic races. It was even said that a 'proportion of the mix of superior and inferior races was said to determine the position of the nation on the scale of superiority and inferiority'. S. Virdee, *Racialized capitalism*.

11 There are a wealth of books advancing this thesis, including; Robin Blackburn, *The Making of New World Slavery: From the Baroque to the Modern, 1492–1800* (Verso, 2010) and Sidney W. Mintz, *Sweetness and Power: The Place of Sugar in Modern History* (Penguin, 1986).

rose with the unimaginable horrors of slavery, its price on the streets of Britain plummeted with every new import, becoming the world's first mass consumer good.

Between 1663 and 1775, the demand for sugar increased by 20 times[12] and sugar came to account for nearly a quarter of all calories consumed in Britain.[13] Beyond its stimulating effects on productivity, the huge imports of sugar and calories meant that the population could grow without more and more people ploughing in the fields of England. And more well fed people meant one thing – more workers for the 'dark satanic mills' of Britain's Industrial Revolution. Just like Warren Buffett and his cans of coke, these sugary beverages also built vast personal fortunes. Britain's first millionaire, William Beckford, acquired his wealth in 1781 at the age of nine after inheriting a slave-run sugar plantation in the Caribbean.[14] The wealth generated by slavery was pumped into funding the technology of the Industrial Revolution: from Watt's steam engine, to the coal and iron industry and the Great Western Railway.[15]

Of the twelve million people who were stolen and trafficked across the Atlantic, it is estimated that Britain was responsible for transporting 3.1 million Africans (of whom 2.7 million arrived).[16] When Britain stopped its formal involvement in the transatlantic slave trade in 1838, there were 46,000 slave owners

---

12 Sidney W. Mintz, *Sweetness and Power: The Place of Sugar in Modern History*.

13 This is about the same calorie intake British people currently take in from sugar today. Jason Hickel, *The Divide: A Brief Guide to Global Inequality and its Solutions* (William Heinemann, 2017).

14 Hilda Kean, 'Where Is Public History?' in *A Companion to Public History*, edited by David Dean (John Wiley & Sons Ltd., 2018).

15 Peter Fryer, *Staying Power: The History of Black People in Britain* (Pluto Press, 2018).

16 www.nationalarchives.gov.uk/slavery/pdf/britain-and-the-trade.pdf, (last accessed 09/2019).

in Britain. The government compensated these owners with one of the largest government bailouts in history – 40 per cent of the government's annual budget at the time. In fact, the loan it took out was so big that the government (and therefore all British tax players) only fully repaid this debt in 2015. The former slaves and their descendants have never received a penny.

'Keep England White'

HMT Windrush sailed into Tilbury Docks, Essex, in June 1948, with around 500 people from Jamaica on board. Following the end of the Second World War, Britain was in serious need of new workers. With hundreds of thousands dead and cities across the country reduced to rubble, Commonwealth citizens were invited to move to the UK and rebuild the motherland. HMT Windrush responded to that call.

While the passengers of the *Windrush* were not the first black people to start a new life in the UK (black Britons had lived on the island for centuries),[17] they were the first to arrive after The British Nationality Act of 1948 had been implemented. The act said that all Commonwealth residents were British citizens and had a right to work in the UK. The new arrivals that stepped onto the shores of Essex were, therefore, as British as Winston Churchill in law – a fact not appreciated by Churchill himself, who complained about the 'considerable' number of 'coloured workers' at the Post Office. When he fought for re-election in 1955, he even suggested to ministers they should adopt the slogan 'Keep England White'.[18] Churchill was not the only one to hold

17 S. Virdee, *Racialized capitalism*.
18 www.theguardian.com/tv-and-radio/2019/jun/24/the-unwanted-the-secret-windrush-files-review-who-could-feel-proud-of-britain-after-this (last accessed 09/2019).

such views. Before the ship had even landed, British officials saw immigration from non-white countries of the Commonwealth as a problem. Even the Labour Party leader Clement Attlee, father of the welfare state, called the new arrivals an 'incursion'.[19]

By the late 1960s, immigration was framed as a national crisis. In 1967 the white supremacist group, the National Front, was established. The following year, Conservative politician, Enoch Powell, famously warned that out of control immigration would lead to social unrest and 'rivers of blood' on the streets. Powell set out three ideas which remain strongly entrenched in the British psyche: that there are too many immigrants, that they are a drain on public services, and that the liberal elite are conspiring to hide this fact from the ordinary British working class. Powell may have been dismissed from the shadow cabinet as a result, but he spoke to a climate of racial hatred and his popularity influenced the Labour government in power, who pandered to his anti-immigrant sentiment. Before the year was over, the Labour government implemented what author Kenan Malik has called the 'most nakedly racist piece of legislation of post-war years':[20] the Commonwealth Immigration Act of 1968. The law was quickly passed to stop non-white Commonwealth citizens from entering the country, a point illustrated most clearly by the Cabinet Secretary at the time, who argued that black and brown immigrants were not 'nationals of this country in any racial sense'.[21]

Anti-immigrant sentiment has from the very beginning been about race and racism. The biggest mass migration to Britain at the time was not from the West Indies, Africa or Asia – it

---

19 Akala, *Natives: Race and Class in the Ruins of Empire*, Two Roads, 2019.
20 www.theguardian.com/commentisfree/2018/mar/04/commonwealth-immigrants-act-1968-racism (last accessed 09/2019).
21 Ibid.

was from the rest of Europe.[22] Yet generally speaking, white immigrants were not seen as a threat or an 'incursion'. Even the *Times* reported in 1968 that the government 'does not any longer profess to believe in the equality of man. It does not even believe in the equality of British citizens. It believes in the equality of white British citizens.'[23]

As the 1970s rolled on, and the National Front marched through the streets, this intolerance was matched by a fierce anti-racist movement. The movement demanded better housing, challenged anti-immigrant policies, monitored the police and fought for better conditions in the workplace. Such was the case during the historic Grunwick Factory strike in 1976. Those on the picket line were not white men in flat caps and overalls – they were predominantly Asian women or as the media called them, 'strikers in saris'. The leader of the dispute, Jayaben Desai, alongside five of her colleagues, walked out in protest at the low pay, lack of union recognition and unfair sacking of a worker at the factory. As she left, she was called a 'chattering monkey' by her manager, to which she replied: 'What you are running here is not a factory, it is a zoo. But in a zoo there are many types of animals. Some are monkeys who dance on your fingertips, others are lions who can bite your head off. We are the lions, Mr. Manager.'[24]

The strike lasted two years, peaking on 11 July 1976, where more than 20,000 protestors crammed into the small back streets of North West London at the factory gates. Despite the Grunwick strike being largely forgotten, this was a key moment in our history. As the whole trade union movement came out in support of the Grunwick strikers, a crowd of 20,000 swelled

22   Akala, *Natives: Race and Class in the Ruins of Empire*.

23   Kenan Malik, *Racist rhetoric hasn't been consigned to Britain's past*.

24   www.bbc.co.uk/news/uk-england-london-37244466 (last accessed 09/2019).

with post office workers, miners, students and dockers. As one Grunwick striker remembers, 'It was an amazing moment because what we had heard about the dockers were that they were racist. They had marched when Enoch Powell had made his inflammatory speeches about rivers of blood. My abiding memory was that these white men had come in solidarity with Asian women in order to protect the idea of solidarity itself.'[25]

This powerful image of multi-ethnic solidarity unfortunately did not last long. To the dismay of the strikers, the union leaders pulled their support following a heavy crackdown by the police (more people were arrested at Grunwick than at any other industrial dispute since the 1920s) and pressure from racist parts of the movement. Despite Jayaben Desai and three others going on hunger strike in protest, the big unions never returned to Grunwick and after two years, the strike ultimately ended in failure. As one of the 20,000 protestors recounted 40 years later, 'the dispute was winnable and defeat was snatched from the jaws of victory'. The defeat cast a long shadow over all working class people in the UK. According to veteran Labour MP Dennis Skinner, what happened at Grunwick was a 'testing ground' for the class battles of the 1980s and the subsequent decline of the trade union movement. Grunwick was one of the first dominos of working class power to fall.

'A really hostile environment'

Feeling ill and having to go to the doctors is one of life's more challenging moments. At least in the UK, the stress and anxiety that sickness brings is cushioned by the knowledge that the healthcare provided by the National Health Service (NHS) is

---

25   www.youtube.com/watch?v=oIrr5e2mHzI (last accessed 09/2019).

free. For the thousands that pass through the doors of hospitals and GPs each day, worrying only about the diagnosis and not the damage to their wallets prevents an untold amount of potential misery.

One person to pass through these doors in 2017 was a 63-year-old man from London called, Albert Thompson.[26] He had received the devastating news that he had prostate cancer and was waiting to start radiotherapy. Upon arrival, rather than being given his treatment, Albert was taken to a side room and asked to provide a British passport. To his utter amazement, he was told that if he couldn't provide the relevant documents, he would have to pay £54,000 for his treatment. Albert Thompson had moved to the UK from Jamaica in 1973. He had worked and lived in Britain all of his life, yet he never had a passport nor needed one. Now he was being told that the NHS was not going to care for him. Why?

It turned out it was not just Albert. Thousands of people across the country who had arrived in the wake of the *HMT Windrush*, having lived in the country for decades, were now being denied hospital treatment.[27] To make matters worse, some of them, including Albert, were even being kicked out of their homes and threatened with being deported 'back' to a country they had little memory of. In 2018, the story hit the news and quickly was termed the Windrush Scandal.[28]

The scandal was the direct result of a calculated tightening of immigration controls in 2012 in order to create, in the words of its architect Theresa May, a 'really hostile environment for

---

26   This is not his real name, but the name he went to the press with.
27   Albert had been the victim of a new change in the law that had only just come in the month before he stepped into the hospital.
28   www.theguardian.com/society/2018/nov/13/cancer-patient-died-after-nhs-demanded-30000-for-treatment (last accessed 09/2019).

illegal migration'.[29] When we think of a border, we probably imagine passport checks at the airport and grumpy guards. The hostile environment has brought the border inland, turning every rental house, hospital and school into a checkpoint. You cannot work, get a driving licence, access free healthcare, rent a home or open a bank account without an immigration check. Every aspect of the government has been turned into a piece of surveillance: doctors and teachers (often against their will)[30] have become the border guards.

While the media call this a 'shocking scandal', in reality the hostile environment is the legacy and logical endpoint of Britain's relationship to race, immigration and class. In the words of leading figure of the American Civil Rights movement WEB Du Bois: 'A system cannot fail those it was never meant to protect.' Immigration and race cannot be separated. If you are white and speak with a British accent, it is highly likely that doctors, teachers or landlords will assume that you are British. If you deviate from this, you become a suspect. According to a recent UN report on the hostile environment, the 'predictable result' of all this has been 'racial discrimination and racialised exclusion'.[31] Even Conservative cabinet ministers upon hearing of Theresa May's plans, predicted that it would discriminate against 'anyone foreign looking'.[32]

In the same way a school gets children to behave through the threat of detention, the government enforces its migration

---

29 The first time Theresa May used the term was in 2012 in an interview with the *Telegraph*.

30 The 'Docs Not Cops' campaign (read more at www.docsnotcops.co.uk) is one example of public service staff resisting against the hostile environment.

31 www.ohchr.org/EN/NewsEvents/Pages/DisplayNews.aspx?NewsID=23073 &LangID=E (last accessed 09/2019).

32 www.theguardian.com/commentisfree/2019/mar/03/the-guardian-view-on-the-hostile-environment-the-right-to-rent-and-other-wrongs (last accessed 09/2019).

policy through the threat of destitution. Theresa May did not invent this idea. She took it from her predecessors: New Labour. In 1999 Tony Blair's government created a separate welfare system for asylum seekers and three years later they were denied the right to work. That same year, the government created 'hit squads' to raid workplaces and homes in the Orwellian search for those without papers. At a time when New Labour were making some progress in the fight against racism with the new anti-discriminatory Race Relations Act, the small print showed that the law did not apply to immigrant enforcement officers.[33] They were exempt.

The relationship between immigration and class is complex. But one of the many lessons we can take away from history is that the undermining of the rights of immigrants and racialised 'Others' is often the first stage of undermining the rights of the wider population. When Labour created a separate welfare system for asylum seekers in 1999, it introduced new tests and conditions that would come to be applied to all welfare claimants under austerity (as we saw in the last chapter).[34] A similar process is underway with the NHS. This is why in 2019, the British Medical Association – the group responsible for representing the interests of doctors – pushed for 'the policy of charging migrants for NHS care to be abandoned and for the NHS to be free for all at the point of delivery'. As one doctor put it, 'charging for some makes it easier to extend charging to the rest of us.'[35]

---

33 www.independent.co.uk/voices/working-class-culture-race-not-as-white-as-you-would-like-to-think-a7903421.html (last accessed 09/2019).

34 For example, support was given only on the grounds that the government could move the person to any area of the country.

35 www.theguardian.com/society/2019/jun/25/scrap-upfront-nhs-charges-for-migrants-says-bma (last accessed 09/2019).

'The ownership of the earth forever and ever'

From housing to prisons to the mines of Marikana, all the chapters of this book have shown how race entrenches class divisions. Society is still structured along deep racial divides that have been created over centuries. WEB Du Bois once said, 'But what on earth is whiteness that one should so desire it? Whiteness is the ownership of the earth forever and ever'. This relationship between whiteness and ownership has not diminished. A recent study of the most powerful financial capitalists in the world found that 84 per cent of them were white.[36] As Reni Eddo Lodge reminds us, this type of 'structural racism' cannot be spotted 'as easily as a St George's flag and a bare belly at an English Defence League rally – it is much more respectable than that'.[37]

Nigel Farage comes from a long line of British elites who have used race as a way to split up the working class: from the invention of whiteness in the tobacco fields of Virginia; to the immigration acts of the 60s and 70s; to the hostile environment. This history reminds us that Britain's so called 'traditional' working class has not always been white. From the Windrush generation, to the 'strikers in saris', the traditional working class is an ethnically diverse group. Structural racism and class inequality has a shared history: we cannot understand race without class or class without race. This is why foremost cultural theorist Stuart Hall said, 'black and white workers have been involved in a common struggle'.[38] To truly overcome the class and racial divisions that

---

36   Peter Phillips, *Giants: The Global Power Elite* (Seven Stories Press, 2018).

37   Reni Eddo-Lodge, *Why I'm No Longer Talking to White People About Race* (London: Bloomsbury Publishing, 2017).

38   Asad Haider, *Mistaken Identity, Race and Class in the Age of Trump* (Verso, 2018), p. 88.

runs through our world, we need a united, anti-racist, working-class movement to fight back against the power of the elite. Many movements across the world right now understand this, and are tearing down racial and class based inequalities in their collective struggle for justice and fairness. While racial inequality goes back hundreds of years, we must remember that it was created and it can be undone.

Chapter 10

Solidarity: Confronting class

Throughout my research for this book, I spoke to a range of young people about what 'class' meant to them. We will finish by drawing together the main themes and arguments discussed so far, with their reflective and memorable words.

'I think class expired a long time ago. Class was in full effect during the 80s and 90s but nobody today really considers themselves to be in a class. Everyone works – even if you are a top employer you still have to go to work every day.' Just like in the introduction to this book, several young people raised the familiar story that class is an outdated and irrelevant concept. But despite repeating this narrative, they actually had a lot to say about class. Through personal stories, they made it clear that class was not simply a historical concept gathering dust, but something that shaped their lives, day in and day out.

Work

'I see myself as working class. My dad works and his job really exploits him. He has to work every single day, he doesn't get any breaks and we have to rely on his income as he is the only person in the family that works. That, in my head, is a working-class person.' Many young people experience the job market through either older family members or work they do themselves, often under precarious, zero-hour contracts:

> It wasn't nice. It was a pharmacy. And you think in a pharmacy you would be doing stuff related to medicines and prescriptions. Which we used to do, but 20 per cent of the time was cleaning. This wasn't what we signed up to when we were offered the job, and we were just being paid the minimum wage. And she expected you to be there – whatever hours she wanted.

'Zero-hour contracts is basically slavery. You do this job but you don't know how many hours you will do it for. You are only going to finish when the guy (or old lady) tells you to finish. I just think zero-hour contracts should be banned.' The insecurity of their own experience was juxtaposed against more secure, professional jobs, highlighting how control over work and the safety wealth brings determines class:

> I would rather be in a lawyer's position than what my dad is in right now – 10 million percent. If I could have a wish, I would do that. Because that is 60k in your account in what, a year? You have a nice house and you feel stable, while when you are an Uber driver you don't feel stable. You feel like you have to do something extra just for stability.

Education

Class does not begin and end with work. Whether it was housing, education, or global inequality, people described how the divides that originate in work, were mirrored in other parts of their lives.

The issue that seemed most pertinent to them was education and the injustice they saw in the schooling system: 'People from private schools, they have that financial backing which means they get their A*s while we are here in state school. Although our brain works the same, we don't have those resources.'

They argued that private schools and elite universities enabled the privileged to get ahead in life, not because it gave them a better education, but because it allowed them to meet the right people:

> Working class people are discriminated against regarding educational institutions like Oxford and stuff, these are all for the elite and they would discriminate against working-class people. This is a social networking place where the elite meet and this is how they maintain the contacts. At the end of the day, if you are favoured, you don't work your way up, you get pulled up.

Housing

As we saw in Chapter 7, housing has been commodified – homes transformed from places to live into places for profit. Many of the students described experiencing the sharp end of this crisis, exposing how inequalities in the housing market entrenched other disadvantages in their lives. As one male student said about getting into university: 'I share a room with my brother, I can't revise properly'. Another person recounted what commodification meant for her:

> My friend had to move her house because she can't afford to live in this area anymore. The commute from her new place is going to be hard and expensive, she comes from a working class family like us, so yeah it does affect our generation,

people just don't talk about it. It was about to happen to my house, but I was lucky.

Global inequality

Class is a global phenomenon and goes way beyond its particular British identity. Many of the young people I spoke to were first, second or third generation migrants and they had a strong sense that their own class identity and experience was shaped by the global inequalities that exist between the Global North and the Global South. In the case below, a student describes how his own class position differs to those back 'home', which in this case was Bangladesh:

> Working class in our country, back home, would be like people riding bikes and rickshaws and stuff. They have to work throughout the day just so they can provide for their families. We have enough money to make sure that we are eating for the next few days. These people have to work everyday so that they can eat. There's a difference between what it is like for us and what it is like for them.

Confronting class

From the quotes above we can see that many young people see class as an arbitrary, unfair and punitive system that works against them. But what, if anything, were people going to do about it?

> We can't do anything. I think as long as the way that society functions, with corrupt people in power making sure people like us don't get what we want. Obviously we want to strive,

we want to get far, we want to get to a high position. They won't let that happen because they are in it for themselves, so unless we can get to the top but we can't. It's not going to happen basically.

Sometimes when it comes to making a change, I just hold back, because its long. We already have to do so much work to get to the position we want to be in, I don't know – I'm just not bothered.

In the face of structural inequality, many young people were pessimistic that things can change. But even those people who started out dejected and apathetic, began to articulate a desire to fight back. And resistance didn't just mean improving their own individual lot in life by working harder and playing the game. They wanted to improve everyone's conditions, and change the rules: 'Even if you work and go up, there will be someone beneath you who has to fill in that role and suffer the same thing you did. So I think that is a good place to start: we fix the jobs we have now and then worry about moving up'.

If you are just going to look for better jobs that's not really going to solve anything, it's just going to make your life harder because nowadays there is higher demand for jobs and who's to say that there is a job for you? Who's there to say that there is a better job for you? Why not just better the job that you have already got? And one day to improve it for those who follow.

In particular, they believed that in order for things to change, people had to come together. Improving jobs, in the words of one student, was 'too difficult just for one person. It will take thousands and thousands of people.' While another drew on the successes of the feminist and LGBTQ+ movement:

> There was the example of gay rights – they still had to make those protests and those active changes to make their voice heard and to have that snowball effect. Or like the suffragette movement, even though they acted aggressively, they had to make their voices loud so that the people and the state would hear them.

The power of collective action, they argued, depended on the strength of solidarity and support between those taking part. With many of the young people I interviewed having grown up in working-class communities, they tended to see solidarity as 'sympathy' for those who shared their background: 'You have sympathy for people when you live in low income areas and you see what people have to do to make a living, to get some money and to feed their family . . . we know the context of their situation.'

Barriers to solidarity

That said, while many people thought that collective struggle based on solidarity was the best way to improve conditions and challenge class inequality, they also described several barriers that stop people from taking action. On the whole, they took the view that piecemeal social change was too slow to actually help deal with the immediate problems in their own lives, with one student saying, 'it would take a long time' and another that it would, 'take years and years' for anything to be achieved. Moreover, they expressed dismay at how the power of the elite seemed so concentrated, entrenched and immovable: 'the people at the top, whoever has inherited property, they are always going to be at an advantage compared to those that don't have that support system'. However, the most consistent and immediate barrier to collective action that I heard was a fear we are all likely to have felt at some point: 'People are quite scared to speak up against their employer for fear of getting fired and their livelihood being taken away.'

'They would just fire you if you opposed, and get someone who would accept it.'

Three ways to help build collective power

The fact that young people bring up these barriers is important. Everything from the fear of losing one's job to the unimaginable power held by the elite, are enough on their own to make us accept the old phrase 'the strong often do as they will and the weak must suffer what they must'. But we must remember that these barriers are neither new nor insurmountable. They have been overcome in the past and can be overcome now. We are often told that the class divides running through our world are inevitable, but as we have seen, many of the benefits that we have today – whether it's holiday pay, the weekend, or the welfare state – have come from people in the past organising collectively to challenge the status quo and demand a better way of life. When faced with systemic injustice, people have always fought back. Whether it is to put a lid on the wealth fizzing up to the super rich, or to challenge the scapegoating narratives blaming immigrants for a crisis they never caused, what we need today more than ever is a strong, anti-racist, feminist, working-class movement. While it's natural to feel despair and fear at times, the best way to challenge such inner and outer turmoil is by collectively standing up for yourself and those around you.

I will finish the book with three practical steps we can all take to shake up our rigid class system, each inspired by points raised by young people during my research for the book.

1. Life-long political education

'Education is the only way out. It can free us of class struggle'. As the modern world is dripping with information, it can be hard to know which films, podcasts, articles, or books to get stuck into. As a starting point, there is a short further reading list at the end of this book to kick things off. But remember: not all knowledge is written down or recorded. Talk to friends and family about the ideas in this book. Everyone has a story to tell and it will undoubtedly be a story that is shaped by class.

2. Join a union

'If there was more advertising of trade unions people would join them'. At school we are never really told about unions and therefore many of us only pick up on them in the media, which 99 per cent of the time frames them in a negative light: unnecessary, selfish, and violent. What this narrative hides is that joining a union brings many benefits: to yourself, your friends, family and colleagues. Unions help with legal advice in the event that your boss has violated your rights. They help you stay informed about changes in the workplace. And most crucially of all – they provide a collective space to effectively demand change. Whether it's striking for better pay or campaigning for better conditions, unions have been the vehicle through which many of our present-day benefits have been secured. And it does not just have to be a trade union in the workplace – there are also renters' unions to stand up against landlords (see resources at the back). If you feel like you are not being given your legally recommended amount of holiday pay, sick pay, breaks or wages, then the best course of action is to get help via a union. And remember – never cross a picket line!

3. Take to the streets

Paint a catchy banner; pack a bag with snacks and water; get out onto the streets and make some noise (remember to bring a whistle, pot and pan, or if you really want, a soundsystem!). If it's your first protest, I would recommend going with friends, as it is much more fun. Whether it's a march, picket line or something more rebellious, there will always be a campaign close by that needs your help. It is only by taking to the streets and organising in our workplaces and communities that we can provide the antidote to the problems we now face, from ecological collapse to in-work poverty. We must remember, as one student reminded me during our discussion, that action inspires further action: 'When we went to the climate strike the other day, you could see that loads of people felt empowered and they were making a change. Feeling that way will motivate you to do bigger things and hopefully, in the end, to change the system.'

Resources

Introduction to class

Charles Umney, *Class Matters: Inequality and Exploitation in 21st Century Britain* (Pluto Press, 2018).

Global inequality

Frantz Fanon, *The Wretched of the Earth* (Penguin, 2001) and *Black Skin, White Masks* (Penguin, 2020).

Pankav Mishra, *From the Ruins of Empire: The Intellectuals Who Remade Asia* (Penguin, 2013).

Jason Hickel, *The Divide: A Brief Guide to Global Inequality and its Solutions* (Windmill Books, 2017).

Work

Kathi Weeks, *The Problem with Work: Feminism, Marxism, Antiwork Politics, and Postwork Imaginaries* (Duke University Press, 2011).

Juno Mac and Molly Smith *Revolting Prostitutes: The Fight for Sex Workers' Rights* (Verso, 2018).

Jamie Woodcock *Working the Phones: Control and Resistance in Call Centres* (Pluto, 2016).

Gender

Dawn Foster, *Lean Out* (Repeater Books, 2016).

Angela Davis, *Women, Race & Class* (Vintage, 2011).

Silvia Federici, *Caliban and the Witch: Women, the Body and Primitive Accumulation* (Autonomedia, 2017).

Money

David Harvey, *Reading Marx's Capital, Volume 1* (Verso, 2010).

RESOURCES

Adam Tooze, *Crashed: How A Decade of Financial Crises Changed the World* (Allen Lane, 2018).

Grace Blakeley, *Stolen: How to Save the World from Financialisation,* (Repeater Books, 2019).

Culture

Owen Jones, *Chavs: The Demonization of the Working Class* (Verso, 2016).

Darren McGarvey, *Poverty Safari: Understanding the Anger of Britain's Underclass* (Picador, 2018).

Sam Friedman and Daniel Laurison, *The Class Ceiling: Why it Pays to be Privileged* (Policy Press, 2019).

The environment

Naomi Klein, *This Changes Everything: Capitalism vs the Climate* (Penguin, 2015).

Andreas Malm, *Fossil Capital: The Rise of Steam Power and the Roots of Global Warming* (Verso, 2016).

David Wallace-Wells, *The Uninhabitable Earth: The Story of the Future* (Penguin, 2019).

Housing

Raquel Rolnik, *Urban Warfare: Housing Under the Empire of Finance* (Verso, 2019).

Lynsey Hanley, *Estates: An Intimate History* (Granta, 2017).

Josh Ryan-Collins, Toby Lloyd and Laurie Macfarlane, *Rethinking the Economics of Land and Housing* (Zed Books, 2017).

The authorities

Frances Ryan, *Crippled: Austerity and the Demonization of Disabled People* (Verso, 2019).

Angela Y. Davis, *Are Prisons Obsolete?* (Seven Stories Press, 2003).

bell hooks, *Teaching to Transgress: Education as the Practice of Freedom* (Routledge, 1994).

Race

Akala, *Natives: Race and Class in the Ruins of Empire* (Two Roads, 2019).

Reni Eddo-Lodge, *Why I'm No Longer Talking to White People about Race* (Bloomsbury, 2017).

Malcolm X, *Autobiography of Malcolm X* (Penguin, 2007).

Solidarity

Jane F. McAlevey, *No Shortcuts: Organizing for Power in the New Gilded Age* (Oxford University Press, 2018).

Pride (2014) – a film about the miners' strike in Britain.

Notes From Below – An online publication about ongoing worker's struggles.

Unions

IWGB – Independent Workers' Union of Great Britain

UVW – United Voices of the World Trade Union

London Renters Union

Know your rights

A good starting resource on your rights in the workplace is Citizen Advice Bureau: www.citizensadvice.org.uk/work/rights-at-work.